THE NEW IQ

INNOVATIVE QUESTIONS

CHRIS COFFEY & DAVID LAM

Foreword by Marshall Goldsmith

author of the *New York Times* and global bestseller
What Got You Here Won't Get You There

For information about this title or to order other books and/or electronic media, contact:
Marshall Goldsmith Stakeholder Centered Coaching
Coach@SCCoaching.com
www.SCCoaching.com

ISBN: 9780986324826 (print)
        9780986324833 (e-book)

Printed in the United States of America

Table of Contents

Foreword

Peter Drucker, the "Father of Management," with whom I was privileged to spend 50 days before his death in 2005, had a great way with words. He distilled meaningful concepts into short phrases more effectively than anyone I have ever met. I was fortunate to be on the Board of the Drucker Foundation (and now the Frances Hesselbein Leadership Institute) for many years. At one of our early Drucker Foundation Board meetings, Peter observed, "The leader of the past knew how to tell; the leader of the future will know how to ask."

Why is asking so important? Almost all of the leaders that I meet manage *knowledge workers*. Peter defined knowledge workers as people who know more about what they are doing than their boss does. It is hard to tell people what to do and how to do it — when they already know more than we do! In today's rapidly changing world, we need to ask, listen and learn from everyone around us.

I wholeheartedly believe this to be true and have experienced this on a near-daily basis for many years as I've traveled the globe speaking to organizations and coaching executives. That's why when Chris and David asked me to write the foreword for *Innovative Questions,* I would have said yes even if Chris weren't my good friend!

I met Chris in 1980 when he was hired to work with my mentor Dr. Paul Hersey at the Center for Leadership Studies, delivering Situational Leadership seminars to IBM and several other Fortune 50 companies. Chris learned quickly how to deliver the content effectively and to make the process interesting and enjoyable for participants. We continued our work together at my firm, Keilty, Goldsmith, and Boone, where Chris delivered the Excellent Manager Program that Frank Wagner and I developed for Fortune 500 Companies. At that time, we were also pioneering the use of 360 feedback, which is so prevalent today.

After many successful coaching engagements, Chris and Frank created a coaching workshop, Stakeholder Centered Coaching, based on my coaching philosophy, and were soon off and running. Hundreds of people have been certified as internal and external coaches in the Train the Coach Certification Workshop, and many internal coaches have been trained in Fortune 500 companies.

For many years, I've encouraged Chris to write and share his experience and knowledge. And he finally has done it, with the help of David Lam, his student from UCLA's Technical Management Program.

What I find so interesting is this book has been written from the student's point of view. David asked Chris questions about his core philosophy of engaging others with innovative questions. Chris and David crafted the book incorporating Chris' philosophy and process as well as David's execution. It's a great premise and an incredibly insightful and entertaining read. The fable is an excellent example, and along with the more "how to" chapters, Chris and David have written a very good book that will help you, your team, and your organization be even more successful.

I hope you'll read it and enjoy it as much as I did!

Life is good.

Marshall Goldsmith

Student's Introduction

This book is a story about my own learning from Chris Coffey. I tell the story all the time because of how it changed my life.

You might think that I'm unique, that, for some reason, the system only works for me. That's not true. Chris has been successfully working with clients for 30 years. He doesn't get paid unless they change for the better.

I met Chris Coffey at UCLA, in an extension program called the Technical Management Program. I was captivated. As someone who had spent years in information technology and security without any formal management training, I was blown away. Could this management mumbo-jumbo work? Could changing your interactions with others change the outcomes? Specifically, in Chris's case, could you ask questions and actually improve what happened next?

I brought Chris in to work with my team. He was highly effective. He didn't use touchy-feely mechanisms. He simply taught us how to assess individual readiness. I brought Chris in again to specifically help us with some issues within the team. We learned to give effective feedback.

I started to go see Chris on a quarterly basis. Working for a non-profit, I wasn't his usual full-blown coaching client, yet he helped me get better each time we got together. It was something akin to business therapy. I would bring him my concerns, and he would give me a new tool to try. And, shockingly, the tool was effective every single time.

We'd been meeting like this for a few years, and I said to Chris, having written articles and chapters on information security, "You need a book." Chris didn't want anything to do with a book, and I nonetheless wrote him the first couple of chapters anyway. It was my turn to be right. Chris saw that you could translate his methodology into words.

So here's the thing: This methodology works. It's crazy how it works. I thought it was amazing when I first started learning with Chris, and it just keeps getting better. The talks that I've had with Chris, some of which are conveyed in this book, have made me so much more effective, it literally staggers me. If you don't believe me, ask my team. The talk around the office when we are having a serious human problem: "What would Coffey do?" All I can say is this: If you are not fortunate enough to be able to hire a top-flight executive coach like Chris, read this book. If you already have an executive coach, read this book. Finally, if you are just having problems with your human interactions, and I know of no one who isn't, read this book. If an IT guy can learn how to amazingly change the course of conversations, so can you.

Introduction

"You know, Allison," Rajesh said, "We have a great team and a great product, but we always seem to be going around in circles. Sales wants one thing, technology wants something else. We can't seem to get anyone to agree. I'm sick and tired of not getting where we say we want to go."

Joe found himself in trouble again: His team insisted that they couldn't complete the new design at all, much less by the deadline. Joe knew better, yet he couldn't convince his lead engineer. Three weeks later, the client dumped the account.

Susan just got the news: She had been passed over once again for a promotion. She kept closing deals, but she was never rewarded.

Sound familiar? Do you wish that you could do something about it? Well, you can. *The New IQ* shows you how to create an environment in which your conversations move in a positive direction. How do you turn your unproductive conversations into productive ones? By simply posing queries using *Innovative Questions* or IQs. Their purpose? To create a *Safe Space* for constructive and positive dialogue.

The roots of our model go back more than two millennia to Socrates and to what scholars call the Socratic Method. Socrates promoted learning, effective dialogue, and debate by asking questions that stimulated thought and necessitated a thought-out response. As perhaps the most well-known question asker, Socrates pioneered asking effective questions. Building on this style, we will teach you the skills to use the types of questions and statements that will help you change the course of your interactions, engage in more productive conversations, and improve the quality of your life and others.

Why this book?

What's different about *Innovative Questions? Innovative Questions* differ from questions you have probably used before in a number of ways. First, they are easy to understand and learn how to use with minimal preparation.

Second, *Innovative Questions* create a *Safe Space* in which your conversational partners can move past an often poisonous stock or programmed response. We will show you how you can help others avoid knee-jerk reactions and instead move toward viable solutions.

Third, using a fable about a fictitious company named Storm Technologies, we will show you the basic operating process for *Innovative Questions:* A process we call *Space Creation. Space Creation* provides the tools to get to the best possible result, at the same time striving to meet the needs of all involved.

We will demonstrate how *Space Creation and Innovative Questions* turn around human interactions, including improving the entire mindset of a discussion, creating clarity without insinuating blame, and allowing win-win outcomes where everyone has participated.

The *Innovative Questions* philosophy follows the thought of Albert Einstein, "Make everything as simple as possible, but not simpler." While we hope that our writing is clear, not everything you read in this book will be easy to implement in spite of being easy to understand. We will specifically address how to overcome some of the difficulties humans have with change and teach you how to overcome your own barriers to change. *Innovative Questions* presents a model that is workable, understandable, and effective, and we will show you how time and time again we've applied these principles effectively and with staggering results.

As we go through this book, we will show you how to make a statement or ask a question relevant to particular types of situations. We advocate a simple process: Identify the situation in the book that matches yours, and try an appropriate question. In turn, you will assist yourself and your team members by allowing them (and you) to get to the best possible outcome.

Finally, this book is written by Chris's student David, who practices these techniques every single day. The tools we present have been used by Chris's clients for over 30 years. This is a real-life methodology already used by many, as we will show through case studies and stories. While it will take your focus and dedication to follow through, the positive outcomes are nothing less than remarkable.

Innovative Question Defined

('i-nə-ˌvā-tiv 'kwes-chən):
Using a question or making a statement to open a *Safe Space* for you and your conversational partners to make better decisions. An *Innovative Question* has the following characteristics:

> It gets people to pause and think.
> It often leads to an 'aha moment.'
> It is focused on getting to an *Ideal Final Result*.

Innovative Questions are very simple. Use a question, make a statement, or use one of the models we've defined to open a space for your conversational partners to make better decisions in reaching each *Ideal Final Result*. By using *Innovative Questions*, not only do you create a more positive perception of you, team members are more able and willing to implement a joint vision and do it happily. Finally, by asking questions that change the perception that others have of you, you will be more readily able to turn conflict into positive outcomes.

Changing Stimulus and Response

Last night, my daughter was talking to me about a friend of hers who was treating her badly. She started hypothesizing, which is a big word for an eight-year-old, about why her friend might be behaving in this way. This was a great opportunity for me to practice parenting using my human skills.

I told her, "We don't know what human beings feel or think. We only see what they do." This has become an important lesson for me as Chris and I wrote this book. It is a basic premise of *Innovative Questions*.

Chris teaches his clients and students that there are only three things that human beings do:

Think
Feel
Behave

Note that we have emphasized "behave." Why? This is a book about human behavior. Behavior is an observable response to a stimulus, an initiating event, which a human being encounters. How we and others behave is the only measure by which others judge us. Since behaviors are the critical element in human interaction, Chris seeks to change behavior for the better.

In response to an initiating event, Human Beings have thoughts. We can have two types of thoughts. Involuntary thoughts are *reactions* to initiating events. Voluntary thoughts, on the other hand, are *responses*. What's the difference? You don't control a *reaction*. It's the consequence of what has happened. In contrast, a *response* is a measured activity that we can control, ideally leading to a productive behavior.

Why is this important? If I can *respond* instead of *react*, I can change the resulting behavior. We can choose to calmly discuss something with our colleagues instead of just reacting and screaming and yelling at them. We've summarized this in the following diagram:

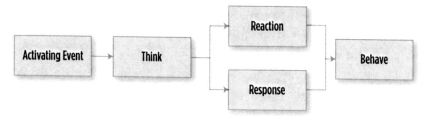

Figure 1.1

Just to be thorough, let's now inject feelings into this equation. I can have a feeling directly related to a thought, and then, that feeling can change after I either react or respond. So, I am not only affecting my behavior as I choose to either react or respond, I'm also affecting my feelings.

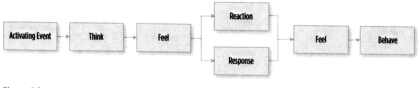

Figure 1.2

An Introduction to Space

Noted management guru Stephen Covey tells his readers that in the process by which human beings respond or react to an initiating event, a space exists between the stimulus (that event) and the response. In this space, human beings can change their normal or knee-jerk *response*.[1]

Covey says that unaware human beings immediately react to a stimulus without any thought. People can learn, however, to find the space between stimulus and response, pause and *respond* instead of *react*.

How can you help guide others to change their reactions to responses? By creating a *Safe Space* in which they can stop, think about what just happened, and *respond* intelligently.

Disruption

How does this work? Changing the words you use causes a *disruption*. A *disruption* is anything that slows down or changes your course. *Disruption* is normally used when we talk about major changes. A *disruption* could be a crisis that causes a company to reinvent itself. And, a *disruption* can also be as minor as changing the words you use.

Words Have Meanings

Words have very specific meanings, and the ways in which you structure your phrases definitively and critically impact your outcomes. You will have better outcomes if you ask specific types of questions that give someone the ability to break the stimulus/response chain.

---

[1] Covey, Stephen R. *The 8th Habit®: From Effectiveness to Greatness.* Free Press. 2004.

Innovative Questions are enablers. They allow for a voluntary change in someone's behavior for the better. As we will show through our explanations, fable, and various case studies, an individual *can* change a *particular* behavior arising from a *certain* stimulus. This beneficial change occurs when *Safe Space* is created. *Innovative Questions* allow us to create just that space.

CHAPTER 2

Cicero

Ability without honor is useless.

— CICERO

Brian McKelvey was a brilliant rainmaker. He was capable of making money for his company in a way that no one had ever seen before. He was right almost all of the time, smarter than just about everyone who met him, and seemed to have an instinct for making the right business decision.

On the other hand, no one wanted to work with him. His bosses found him abrasive and arrogant. Behind closed doors, his peer team members talked of taking him to the parking lot and giving him a good beating. And, at happy hour, his subordinates complained how they would leave the company except for their amazing bonuses.

In years of work with his clients, Chris has found this to be a common scenario. A bright and productive individual is unable to lead because of how he or she interacts with others. The *Innovative Questions* model has helped these people, and it can help you as well. Before going any farther, there are some ground rules, so let's set the stage for success with *Innovative Questions*.

Innovative Questions require that you approach each situation and individual based on a moral foundation. Over 2000 years ago, Cicero detailed just such a view of a leader, including the following two critical qualities:

1. A bedrock of principles.
2. A strong moral compass.

Innovative Questions work repeatedly only when the person asking the questions follows Cicero's two points. Before anything else, a foundation must exist such that the questioner is guided by a moral compass. On top of these principles, each action you take must be in accordance with societal mores for how individuals want to be treated.

Clearly, we are not alone in citing a value-based approach to working well with others. Over the last decade, we have seen an increasing consensus in management books that strong values increase a manager's ability to lead a team. These values also manifest themselves in an earnest desire for another person to succeed, almost always translated by a team's feeling that their manager supports them. Managers who do not support their teams can find it difficult to get their support in return.

Story: Do You Want to Help Me?

Here's an example. When David would coach IT Directors, he would often hear complaints from the team members. For example, people just hate Fred:

> *Fred is not at all interested in helping me; he comes for just the minimum number of required hours, leaves at six, and that's it. And, whenever I ask Fred for help, he's never available. He always has some excuse.*

On the flip side, people really love Peter.

When Peter needs people to stay late on a project, he is right there in the trenches next to them. If they are upset about something, he's willing to talk to them any time, day or night. He cares about getting the job done, and he cares about each member of his team.

Managers and leaders should also realize that even if they think their moral compass is in the right place, they can be perceived as being in the wrong place. For example, managers who make long personal calls every day may think that they are doing a fine job, and their teams still may feel let down.

Story: The Long Lunch

Armand was working with Sally on completing an important project. They were putting together an advertising campaign for an important client, and Armand was burning the candle at both ends. He worked late every night and on weekends.

Sally, on the other hand, was coming in late consistently, taking two-hour lunches every day, not doing her piece of the project by approving campaign materials in a timely manner, and was difficult to reach when urgent approvals were needed. When Armand tried to talk to Sally, she became defensive.

Sally thought that she was a good manager — that she was working hard and there for her staff. In reality, she was rationalizing her behavior and not thinking about the impact it had on others. By taking advantage, Sally was affecting her team's ability to do their jobs well and without stress. On another level, her taking advantage was plain old not fair, which triggers many reactions in the brain, and that just made everyone feel even worse.

Intentions

Whether or not it is your intention to take advantage of a situation, if a person perceives that you are not doing the right thing or not being fair, they are going to be frustrated with you. "A bedrock of moral principles" means that your team feels and perceives that you are a fair player and that you have their best interests at heart. Without that, it's going to be very difficult to get them to feel safe with you and collaborate alongside you.

Safe Space

As we discussed in the previous chapter, to get the very best behavior from human beings, you must create a space in which they can respond thoughtfully instead of reacting. We refer to this space as *Safe Space*. The words of each *Innovative Question* are designed specifically to create *Safe Space*. That, however, wins only part of the battle. Before any *Innovative Question* has any chance of working, you must conduct yourself in a way that allows people to feel safe with you.

For example, if your dialogue with others even remotely signals humiliation or demeans someone else, you will not succeed with *Innovative Questions*. Our methods work only when people feel psychologically safe to come out of their habitual reactions and work collaboratively with others.

Since most people are plenty smart enough to pick up that they are being manipulated, managers who attempt to manipulate others will also not succeed with *Innovative Questions*. *Innovative Questions* are not manipulative. They create an environment in which people, with your help, get to the best possible decision. They are able to do this because they believe they are treated fairly, have their concerns heard, and find their point of view repeatedly understood and fairly considered.

Consistency

Similarly, managers who are not consistent with what they say or do not keep their promises to their team will find themselves struggling to retain people and keep them committed and happy. No one likes being told one thing one day and another the next. Even worse, when a manager changes his or her mind and chastises the team for doing what they were instructed to do in the first place, morale drops in an instant.

Respect

Innovative Questions also require respect between individuals. Chris has encountered many top-level leaders who don't respect others and, as a result, have run into many interpersonal issues. As an example, a number of these leaders will ask people for their opinions and then completely ignore those perspectives. This just makes people frustrated. *Innovative Questions* just do not work when respect is not part of the equation.

Not Needing to Win

Additionally, Chris has found that high-level, highly intelligent managers have a strong desire to win. Winning at any cost comes at a high price, whereas allowing others to win as well brings with it great benefits. It's important to allow others to win as often as you can.

The Importance of Your Interactions

We'd like to suggest to our exceptional managers that you need to be aware of your need to win. There are two issues that we've seen repeatedly arise in these circumstances. First, never letting the other person win demoralizes that person. Second, while you may have a better solution, the price of that better solution may be too high. You should ask yourself if your idea is in actuality that much better than the other that it's worth demoralizing the person who brought you a different option — especially if the idea is only a little bit less optimal than yours. Is pushing your "little bit better" idea worth losing the energy of that individual? Or, could you leverage this opportunity and build another partner in executing your vision? Here's an example:

> *Once again, Jason was the recipient of angry feedback from one of his staff members. "You never listen to us! It's always your way or the highway. Why can't you just let one of us run with our ideas? We are sick and tired of not getting to work on our ideas!*

In this instance, Jason didn't have partners or team members. He had worker bees. He was telling them what to do and they were angry about it. All of their good thought work turned into nothing.

We encourage all leaders and managers to think about the way your actions are perceived and perhaps spend a few minutes thinking about how each interaction went. We will discuss this in greater depth in our chapter on After Action Reviews. Each and every interaction with an individual is important and helps you along the road of doing better with your team and other colleagues.

Why Innovative Questions?

Innovative Questions focus on improving your journey toward a desired outcome and getting to the best possible outcome. When you come from a place of supporting others and a commitment to values, the journey is not only enjoyable, you facilitate getting optimal results. Because *Innovative Questions* work only when people are safe enough to come out of their normal patterns, leaders and managers must create a psychologically safe environment. Starting with Cicero's bedrock of principles provides an important starting point for creating *Safe Space*.

CHAPTER 3

Clarity

On top of Cicero's foundational principles, leaders have to effectively communicate to others. In his course on effective communication skills, Dalton Kehoe tells his students that while talk is automatic, effective communication is a skill that can be taught and learned.[2]

Kehoe talks about a number of important things that must occur during communication. Critically, the leader must effectively convey his or her point of view. Additionally, the other person or people in the communication must walk away feeling good about the process. Just as Cicero pointed out, without a foundational element, communication starts to fall apart.

Before we get into the model for *Innovative Questions* in our fable, we want to first touch on the ideal outcome for any business decision. We refer to this outcome as the *Ideal Final Result*. If you will, the *Ideal Final Result* is the Holy Grail of the management process. It is the ultimate outcome defined by following a deliberate process and including all stakeholders.

---

[2] Kehoe, Dalton, *Effective Communication Skills*. Chantilly, VA: The Teaching Company, 2011. Available at *www.thegreatcourses.com*.

Clarity goes hand-in-hand with the *Ideal Final Result*. *Clarity* is the process of specifically driving toward what you want to achieve and defining in advance how you are going to get there. Clarity is a process; the *Ideal Final Result* is the outcome.

In repeated discussions between the authors, with our staffs and our clients, we've come to the same conclusion: *Clarity* empowers us. Lack of *clarity* invariably brings unclear expectations, unclear commitment, the failure to assign reasonable resources, and, in many cases, an entirely different end result than we were expecting.

Words Are Powerful

Innovative Questions are premised on the tenet that words are powerful. Words can change how people think about things, and they can change the way people behave. For example, let's look at two different phrases:

1. Outcome
2. *Ideal Final Result*

In our experience, *outcome* is blasé and vague. *Ideal Final Result*, as we define it, has *clarity* and shared meaning. Let's explore this further by taking a look at a case study.

Knee-Jerk Reactions

People knee-jerk in response to the word *outcome* and thus don't spend any real time thinking about it. Here's an example:

CFO: What's the outcome you are trying to have for the sales department?

Sales Manager: We want to make sales.

Now, let's change the words up. Here's the way it goes now:

CFO: I want to gain clarity on what *Ideal Final Result* you need to achieve for the sales department.

Sales Manager: Final result? Now let me think about that...

If this appears to be too simple, it's not. Our experience has shown that the difference between these two examples is dramatic. Why don't you try it out? It's a simple change, and you can see for yourself how powerful these words can be.

Six Questions of Clarity

With *Innovative Questions*, we achieve clarity by applying the following six questions:

1. What is the *Ideal Final Result?*
2. How do we define success?
3. What measurements will we use along the way?
4. What resources are there?
5. Who is accountable for what?
6. What are the consequences/rewards for failure and success?

Asking, Not Telling

Another important point of *Innovative Questions* is asking instead of telling and asking the right questions in the right way. Before we go down each of the six questions of clarity, we want to talk about the importance of asking questions. That means, as leaders, we don't just tell what we want. Remember, *clarity* is a process leading to an outcome. *Clarity* is not a one-way street. Both parties involved in defining an outcome need to be engaged. When both parties are interested in *clarity*, they ask questions of each other to get to the *Ideal Final Result*. Let's take a look at the six questions now.

Ideal Final Result

Remember, the *Ideal Final Result (IFR)* represents the ultimate goal we are trying to attain. By defining the goal up front and supporting it with clarifying questions, we have a much better chance of getting where we want to go. Perhaps more importantly, because we define the *IFR* with our stakeholders, everyone knows the end result for which we are striving.

Success

Once we have defined the *Ideal Final Result,* we need to define what success looks like. People aren't necessarily used to thinking with specificity about this, so they tend to pause and put more thought into it. Success brings up different connotations into our minds than "outcome" or even "result." Asking the right question forces our mind to think differently.

Measure

Once we define what success looks like, we need to think about how to measure it. Again, people don't always think about measuring, so with this *Innovative Question,* they pause, they truly think about it, and they come up with measurement systems that help them refine their *Ideal Final Result* in the first place.

Resources

Understanding what resources are needed enables us to think further about exactly what is required to succeed. We have found that many people just jump in without thinking about what resources are going to be necessary for success. Defining the resources upfront also helps us gain further clarity on the process we will follow on the road to the *Ideal Final Result*.

Accountability

Accountability defines who is going to do what. Accountability helps us not only define what human resources are needed for project success, it wakes up those individuals who are participating because they are individually accountable for a particular outcome. Additionally, when people are held accountable, everyone needs to pull their own weight. Teams often express frustration when their managers don't support them by ensuring that everyone does their share.

Consequences

Understanding the consequences and rewards of achievement helps us prioritize our individual tasks as we are working toward an *Ideal Final Result*. We achieve additional clarity with these last three questions: Resources, accountability, and consequences. Since people aren't used to thinking forward, these questions allow individuals to think ahead, get out of their immediate knee-jerk reactions, and put together a much better solution.

Conclusion

Clarity and *Ideal Final Result* create a foundation for more positive outcomes simply because we define upfront both the outcome and a path to success. The equation is simple: By spending time upfront to achieve *clarity*, individuals are able to spend more time focusing on their interactions with others rather than on trying to figure out what exactly they need to do at each turn of events. How many times have you run around like a mad person trying to adjust to a new question that *just* came up about what you are trying to get done? Think about how much better things could be if you instead focused on an *Ideal Final Result* and already knew how you were going to get there. Indeed, once your team understands what the *Ideal Final Result* looks like, they can work together in a far more coherent fashion to drive toward that goal.

CHAPTER 4

Space Creation

In this next section, we present the foundational process for our *Innovative Questions* methodology. We call this process *Space Creation*. Because *Space Creation* contains many working parts, we chose to create a fictional story — a fable — in which we present our ideas. In the fable, we show how the team at a fictional company named Storm Technologies uses *Space Creation* with *Innovative Questions* as they grapple with an issue critical to the continued existence of the company.

While the explanation of the strategy behind *Innovative Questions* is more complicated than the method itself, we both firmly believe that you should understand the underlying tenets before you move on to practicing *Innovative Questions*. Specifically for that reason, we've created the following fable to illustrate these basic tenets.

CHAPTER 5

The Storm and the Calm: A Fable

John Adamson was the new CIO for Storm Technologies, an up-and-coming challenger to veteran web companies Amazon and Google, Storm Technologies offers a way for people to inexpensively and easily do all of their work on the Internet as opposed to needing to install programs or servers in their offices or homes. John was recruited by the CEO of Storm, Rajesh Haneev, who was his college roommate. Rajesh was a brilliant visionary and had lobbied for a long time to bring on his friend as a right-hand man to execute his vision of an evolved and more stable company.

John was able to recruit two of his former staff members to join him at Storm Technologies. Lucy Weingart had a solid track record as a project manager and a great way with people. Peter Ankersmythe was a brilliant technologist and always "able to solve the problem." At the end of their first day at Storm, Rajesh brought together key players on his team to introduce them to John, Lucy, and Peter as well as talk about the strategic direction for the company.

Rajesh kicked off the meeting. "Everyone, I'd like to introduce you to John Adamson, Lucy Weingart and Peter Ankersmythe. As you know, John will be our new CIO, and his key players are Lucy and Peter."

Although Storm Technologies was riding a wave as a secure alternative to Amazon and Google via their proprietary technology called SecurePad, they were starting to run into some issues as the two behemoth providers were catching up to them. Storm was able to win deal after deal because they enabled people to secure their critical computer data effectively. No other company could even come close to the level of security that Storm provided. Unfortunately for Storm, Amazon and Google were now beginning to offer competing solutions, albeit offerings that were less secure.

Rajesh now turned the meeting over to Devon Singer, the primary architect of SecurePad. "As you clearly know, Storm is a cloud provider. A cloud provider offers services to individuals and companies which exist entirely on the Internet. This means that an individual only needs a web browser and an Internet connection in order to access a cloud technology. Everything else lives on our servers and networks. We take all the work out of what they need to do and make it easy for them to get their work done." Devon continued, "Unfortunately, the biggest problem with Internet technologies lies in the password protection. As we have seen with recent Internet attacks, once a hacker has taken control of a user's machine, they have full access to that machine. Furthermore, everything that has been tried to protect a single computer has been defeated. And once someone has full control of a single machine, they also own all the passwords that were saved on it.

"Our solution, SecurePad, uses a touchscreen device such as an iPad or Android Tablet to allow people to securely connect to our system simply by moving their hand over the screen. Using our proprietary technology, we create a secure link between the computer, the tablet, and our system. Hackers have not been able to figure out how to defeat our technology. Even though we are the talk of all of the hacker discussions, no one has any idea how to get around our multiple protections.

"Our competitors, unfortunately, have begun marketing their supposedly secure systems. While these alternatives are not nearly as secure as ours, they are starting to impact our sales."

Devon turned the meeting over to Allison Winker, the vice president of sales and marketing. Allison started with, "We have begun losing some large accounts because they prefer going with one of the big names. We are also having some problems because, when we talk to non-technical individuals, they fail to understand our value proposition. Exacerbating the situation, we have not been able to effectively demonstrate and build a convincing and compelling argument for laypeople as to why our system offers a significantly better solution. We need to find a persuasive way to continue to win sales and retain customers."

Rajesh nodded his head in agreement with what Allison was saying. He turned to his new CIO. "John, you and I go back for some time. We've had some great discussions since college about how to steer my vision. I'm excited that we are finally having the opportunity to formally work together." Even though Adamson was brought in as the technology guru for the company, the group knew he had a strong entrepreneurial spirit and an ability to solve complex non-technical problems. All eyes turned to him.

John was ready. "It's going to take me some time to fully understand this challenge, including both the threats and the opportunities that it presents, and I am going to need your help for that. I'd like to propose that, together, we define a process by which we can achieve a good decision. In one of my previous companies, we brought in an executive coach, who helped us define a roadmap to getting to an ideal decision point. I'd like to use that process here."

John continued, "Before we go any further, I'd like for us to think about what our *Ideal Final Result* might look like — 'What are we trying to accomplish?' Only then, after we have defined this outcome, can we ask the question, 'How are we going to get there?'"

Allison answered his question right away. "Well, our desired outcome is easy: We want to close sales."

John looked at her, pausing for a moment. He asked her back, "Are you sure? Is that the best answer? Is it possible that another answer exists that more accurately describes what we want to achieve in the end?" Alison's eyes widened. John could tell she was ready to hear more.

"Before I ask the group some questions, I have a cautionary request for Rajesh. My coach always cautions managers and leaders to be careful of the trap of framing. Just because you, as leader, think you know what the outcome should be does not mean that you put that out there upfront. First, your team may pick up that you are trying to steer toward a particular outcome. Second, you will lose the opportunity of having a fresh set of eyes create an even better solution than what you were thinking of in the first place. Rajesh, are you okay with that?" Rajesh thought about John's request for a second and then nodded.

"Okay, let me ask the group a question. How much time have you thought about the ideal result at which you want to arrive?" He looked around the room to a set of blank stares. "That's what I thought. Many times, we just 'knee-jerk' in response to a question. We need to think about it. And, how do you ensure we think about it? We create a space that allows just that.

"Together we are going to go through a process that my coach refers to as *Space Creation*. *Space Creation*, first, allows us to effectively define the *Ideal Final Result* and then gives us a means and a place to make competent moves toward achieving that result."

John could see everyone was tired and not fully grasping the concept, so he said, "Since it's almost the end of the day, I'd like to propose the following. Take my challenge home with you and put some thought into the *Ideal Final Result* for Storm. In the morning,

I'll outline the details of *Space Creation,* and we can work through the process to an outcome. Sound okay?" Everyone nodded in assent. "Good," John said. "Any questions, comments, or concerns?" John paused to look around. No one was ready to react just yet. "Great; then, I will see you all first thing in the morning back here."

The Next Day

The next day, they met in the conference room again. Rajesh, the CEO, started off the conversation. "I spent all evening thinking about your challenge, John. I think you're right. I think that we should work on deciding where we want to go first. This sounds like a wise process."

John started back in. "Good, I'm glad to hear that. Here's what I'd like to propose. Let me explain the process a little bit, and then we can get underway. Sound okay?"

The Three Skills

Since there were unanimous smiles and nods around the room, John got underway. "Okay, let me first start at the 40,000-foot level and talk about three skills that we, as managers and leaders, need to succeed." John paused and took a deep breath. "First, we need to be able to make decisions. If we don't make a decision, we will not get to an outcome. Second, in the process of making those decisions, we need to be able to deal with the conflict that inevitably and, this is important now, necessarily arises in a healthy environment. That's not to say there isn't conflict in a dysfunctional environment. It's just not necessarily useful or healthy conflict.

"Third, because we are individuals with opinions as well, we need to be able to *fairly* convey our point of view and *fairly* influence the outcome. That doesn't mean we shove our opinions down the throats of others. That would not be appropriate or skillful. It is critical that we appropriately inject our opinions into the conversation. Do you agree with these three statements: Make decisions, deal with conflict, and inject our opinions?"

Allison raised her hand, and, when John nodded to her, she said, "I think I see where you're going, but I'd like to hear more."

"Okay," John replied, "let me do it this way. I'm going to talk a little bit more about *Space Creation* and then work through these three skills. Sound okay?" Everyone nodded.

How *Space Creation* Works

"Okay, let me talk about the process through which we achieve these goals. *Space Creation,* which I define as creating a *Safe Space* in which human beings can safely, efficiently, and effectively work together to achieve an *Ideal Final Result,* has multiple working parts. Let me put up this diagram and go through and explain it.

"Human beings have developed shortcuts for processing the immense amount of data that they need to look at each day about which they need to make decisions. Not only that, but they are stuck in a rut. To quote Marshall Goldsmith, inertia is the default human state. That means that we are automatically at a disadvantage when we are trying to get a group of people to make a decision. Why? Simply put, most people react to a typical question with a habitual, preprogrammed response.

"We need to change that. We need to create a space in which people don't need to knee-jerk, in which they can break out of their inertia and change directions, and in which they can come out of some of their protective coverings and frankly discuss where they want to go, why they want to go that way, and what else they are thinking.

"Before we move into the process portion of *Space Creation,* we need to discuss its foundations. The basic foundational element of *Space*

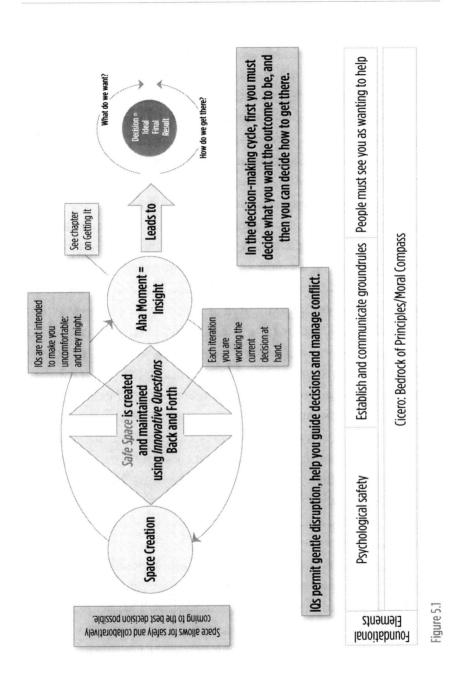

Figure 5.1

Creation is what Roman philosopher Cicero, born in 106 BC, referred to as a bedrock of principles. One cannot create a safe environment without understanding that the people around the room, in particular, the leader, are fair players with their interests at heart. This leads to another foundational element of *Space Creation:* If people don't see you as wanting to help them be successful, *Space Creation* becomes ineffective.

"There are two other foundational elements I want to make sure are on the table before diving into *Space Creation.* First, the environment must be one of psychological safety, where people feel safe to speak their mind, and second, the ground rules of that environment need to be communicated in advance. Without these four foundational elements, everything else falls apart. Does this make sense?"

John stopped for a moment and looked around the room. He seemed to have everyone's attention as they all nodded slowly at him. John continued, "Once we have this foundation of principles, we can talk about actual *Space Creation. Space Creation* changes the context in which questions are asked or answered. Instead of engendering a knee-jerk reaction without thought, *Space Creation* allows for a thoughtful response and consideration of other perspectives.

"I'm going to start out with a very basic ground rule and then dive in to illustrate the *Space Creation* concept. Let me start with this principle — there will be no use of the word 'but' at all in our conversations. 'But' is a word that diminishes the value of a contribution that someone else has made, and it is contrary to a bedrock of principles. It is verboten."

Peter, the technology guy, had a question. "But what if somebody has a really stupid idea? I mean one that has no chance of flying."

John responded, "Pete, that's a good question. The answer is simple. In innovative companies, many ideas which seemed on the surface to be idiotic or impossible ended up being part of the final great idea. Let's not squash the idea before we get it on the table and have a chance to get it thoroughly vetted. Additionally, as I just mentioned, I want everyone to feel safe to put their ideas on the table. If the first response to a wacky idea is to squash or demean it with words or body language, we might not get an unconventional idea that works out. Take SecurePad, for example. Imagine if someone would not put that great idea on the table because they worried that they would be ridiculed. What if somebody told Devon that SecurePad would never fly? That tablets were too expensive to use as an authentication device and that it just wouldn't work. Maybe it wouldn't have gone any further, and maybe Storm Technologies wouldn't be what it is today. Does that make sense?"

The group nodded their heads in agreement. They seemed to like how this was going. "One more point," John added. "A seemingly crazy idea can lead to a different, great idea. The purpose of *Space Creation* is to allow for a safe exchange of ideas and can lead to results that are well beyond what anyone expected. *Space Creation* also challenges everyone to think more openly." John paused, "Are we all good?" John looked around. Everyone was still paying attention and nodding their heads. A good sign. John smiled and then continued, "Okay, let's get started with some of our work, and I'll walk you through the *Space Creation* process as we go. Let's begin by throwing out ideas for where we want to go and writing them up here on the computer board."

Lucy was grinning a mischievous smile as she raised her hand and said, "I think we should be the McDonald's of the cloud provider world."

Even before she finished, Peter was all over this. "Come on, guys, let's be serious. Is that how we want to have the session go?"

John finished writing the statement on the computer board and turned to the group. "Okay, let me make sure we are crystal clear on the ground rules. Negative commenting on another person's idea destroys the creation of space. No buts, no come-ons, no rolling of the eyes. I'm going to show you in a few minutes how to provide input while keeping our *Safe Space* intact.

"Is everyone on the same page with me?" John looked around the room and everyone was nodding. Everyone except Peter. Peter sat there with his arms crossed, looking angry. John looked directly at him and said, "Peter, what's bothering you? Spit it out." Peter said, "I'm not into this game-playing stuff. We have a big problem, and we need to solve it now. How can we put a stupid idea on the table and not tell the person that it's a stupid idea — I didn't come to this company to fail."

John responded, "Folks, I'm going to step outside for a minute and talk to Peter. Would you all take 10?"

John walked down the hall to his office with Peter. He didn't talk to Peter while they were walking, and somehow John didn't look angry. He had a calm smile on his face. "Have a seat, Peter." Peter sat down hard, looking like a petulant child, with his arms crossed tightly and a frown on his face. John continued with a compassionate look and tone, "We've worked together for many years. I know you're not into what you call the touchy-feely stuff. That said, your outburst before was not helpful at all. I would appreciate some leeway while I propose this new system here. What's bugging you?" John paused while he collected his thoughts. He continued, "We've tried revolutionary systems before — you've had an open mind. And... this is a new place: this is no way to introduce yourself to the team. Frankly, I'm concerned about your comments."

Peter replied, "I don't know what's gotten into you, John. Why are we using this new system? It used to be we could just put down some good solutions and get going." "Because," John said, "I've learned a better way. By putting everything on the table, without framing the problem or solution in advance, we have a better chance of getting buy in from the group and developing the best *Ideal Final Result* when we make our decision. Now, you've known me for a long time, so can I count on your support while we go through the process? I promise, you can have all the 1:1 time with me you would like to debrief and/or vent after we do it."

John looked earnestly with a smile on his face at Peter while he was chewing it over. Peter said, "Okay, only for you." John then responded, "Can I make a suggestion, Peter?" In response to the nod he got, John continued, "I think you need to go in there and apologize to everyone else, especially Lucy. You're making a name for yourself, and this is not the way to do it."

"Okay," answered a reluctant Peter.

When the group reconvened, before he took his seat, Peter said, "I want to apologize to the group. I'm not always the most patient person, and my outburst wasn't appropriate. I promise to do better."

John started up again, "Peter, thanks for saying that. Okay, let's get back on track. Now, who's next with an idea?"

One by one, the group members shouted out their thoughts. John wrote down the brainstorming ideas on the *Ideal Final Result*:

- Become the McDonald's of cloud providers.
- Ensure profitability for our stakeholders by giving our users a great product.
- Be the Nordstrom of cloud computing.
- Provide out of this Earth cloud computing.
- Bring great value and security to our cloud customers.
- Change the computing paradigm for individual businesses by providing exceptional service and products one client at a time.

The list went on to fill the entire board.

John said, as they were reaching lunch time, that they had done great work. Only once had someone tried to provide negative feedback on an idea, and several members of the group, not John, reminded them that they weren't providing feedback yet. They were going to learn that in the next step. Once, Peter used the word "but." It was immediately brought to his attention by the rest of the group, and he replaced the "but" right away.

The group decided that they should go out for Chinese food at a local restaurant. There was a great buzz in the air, as the forming team excitedly talked about some of the ideas they had thrown out. John just sat back and let them talk. He knew the next part of the lesson was coming.

▦   ▦   ▦

When they returned to the conference room, John addressed the group. "Now I'm going to teach you how to express your opinion in a way that supports *Safe Space* and keeps it intact. Obviously we can't just throw out ideas and let them go forward. That would be pointless. We have to get to a point where we can decide if these ideas have any merit.

"At this point, let me introduce you to another concept, *Innovative Questions*. So before actually introducing the concept, let me ask the group a question. What's the normal state of the human condition?"

Lucy raised her hand. "I remember," she said. "It's inertia. People keep going in the same direction that they are already going in."

"That's absolutely correct, Lucy," John replied, "and our job as leaders is to get them to change that."

John asked, "What's the normal way that we do this?"

Rajesh answered for him. "We tell that person that they are wrong."

"Absolutely correct," John responded, "Do you think that's effective?"

Peter decided to chime in. "Why isn't it effective? We are all adults. Why can't I tell someone else my opinion?" It was clear Peter was trying to ask the question in a nice way.

"Because," John answered, in a tone appropriate for a patient father of a young child, "there's a lot of complex machinery going on in a person's mind, and when you tell them they are wrong, and they already have inertia in the direction they're going, they aren't even *thinking* about changing their mind."

Peter thought about this for a minute and decided to hear some more. He nodded his head as a signal for John to continue. "Okay," John said, "I can see the team is ready for the next step. Let me go back to the diagram (Figure 5.1) and reiterate where we have been with this model. On top of Cicero's bedrock of moral principles, we have psychological safety, ground rules and 'people must see you as wanting to help' as foundational principles. These four principles allow for *Space Creation*. To get to the next step, we now create the actual *Safe Space* using *Innovative Questions*. To demonstrate how this works, I'm going to present the quintessential *Innovative Question*. Someone give me a statement that may be controversial."

Allison raised her hand. When John nodded at her, she said, "Global warming is ruining our planet."

"Excellent," John replied. "Is it possible that the opposite of what you are saying is true?"

John could see that he had confused everyone in the room. And he smiled a knowing smile because he obviously expected it. "I'll repeat the question," he said. "Is it possible that the opposite of what you are saying is true?"

He continued, "That's right, you heard me correctly. I'm asking you to think about whether or not the opposite of what Allison said is true." In response to a set of confused faces, John said, "Let me map this out so it's a bit clearer. Normally, we make intuitive judgments about whether or not something is right or wrong, or if it makes sense to us or not. We create these heuristic shortcuts because we make so many decisions that we just learn what to say yes to and what to say no to. This is a problem because taking that shortcut doesn't allow you to carefully consider a question.

"To break that habit, you need to ask someone to look at something from another perspective. And that means trying to turn something around and look at it, in a different way. Make sense? Questions?"

Allison started first. "What you're saying is very difficult to do. How can I defend the opposite side of my position?"

John replied, "Exactly! It is hard. And, you know what? You can. More importantly, you can help other people do just that, and completely and utterly change the nature of conflict management and making decisions." John paused for dramatic effect as he let this cornerstone idea sink in.

"Let's break this down further. Allison, in your statement about global warming, you said that 'global warming is ruining the planet,' correct?" Allison nodded. "Okay," John continued, "What is the opposite position?"

Allison thought about it for a minute, and then said, "Okay, that's easy — global warming is not ruining the planet." "Good," John said, "that's one potential interpretation. Excellent. Might there be any part of the opposite position that you might agree with?"

Allison thought for a second and then said, "Well, I suppose that global warming could lead to more mild winters."

John smiled a large, engaging smile and said, "Exactly! So what happened with this question? First, you had to stop and think. Second, you thought of a different possibility. And, I'm going to put out there that you did that without feeling defensive, putting up walls, or trying to make arguments for your position. Is that correct?"

Allison started nodding, slowly at first, and then she smiled while she got it. "Wow," she said, "that makes sense. That's amazing."

"Let me summarize what we just learned about *Innovative Questions*, or IQs:

1. IQs create a *Safe Space* for constructive and positive dialogue.

2. IQs create a space in which your conversational partners can move past an often poisonous stock or programmed response.
3. IQs allow for finding common ground (what everyone can agree on).

"Let me continue with one more point, and then we can get to my next exercise. A critical point of *Innovative Questions* is asking instead of telling and asking the right questions in the right way. As we work through our current decision at hand, I will introduce new IQs that will help you get the hang of this." As he saw some eyes widen, John paused and then continued, "Stick with me — you'll see that it's actually pretty easy." John could tell he hadn't completely sold the group yet, so he gave them a big smile and continued.

"Here's the fun part. Let's each take a look at the list we created just a little while ago and pick the one we disagree with the most. That will give you some practice at looking at the opposite side of your view."

Not surprisingly to John, Peter was the one who raised his hand. "John, I know that I told you I would go along with this, but this is over the top. I think I'm going to struggle defending something I don't agree with." Everyone in the room nodded.

Except John, who said, "You will be surprised at how easy it can be when you don't have to be right. And one of the things we will learn through this process is that being right is not the outcome you are looking for. It's making the best decision. 'Being right' is poisonous to *Safe Space*."

John continued, "May I suggest as a first step that, as you consider each idea, look for what part you do agree with. Here's some background. Since your brain is going to look for things that agree with your world view, it is naturally going to find that with which you disagree. We call these 'cognitive biases.' Let's get around those. Let's turn your brain around. To that end, let's make this another one of our ground rules: look for what you agree with.

"Remember, the purpose of this exercise is to build the ability to look at another possibility. I'm challenging you and everyone else in this room to turn around your perspective and think about whether or not it's possible that the opposite of what you are thinking is true."

John looked around the room and could see there was some skepticism in the air. "I'll tell you what," John said, "let's give it a shot, and if anyone either dies or collapses, we will stop immediately." The group laughed, except Peter. John could tell he was both uncomfortable and a little bit frustrated. However, knowing that Peter would come around, John kept the exercise going.

■ ■ ■

One by one, each person went through their presentations, supporting ideas with which they were uncomfortable. John could tell that Peter was struggling to come up with some reasons to support the McDonald's idea, and, in the end, even he at least had a few, including: Defining an international brand name that everyone recognizes; having a consistent level of safety and quality; and knowing that you can always get a decent cup of coffee.

When everyone in the group had had a chance to add their input, John asked a concluding question, "Okay, did anyone learn anything?" Everyone was nodding their heads.

Lucy started talking first. "I have to say, this was definitely eye-opening. That is, being forced to take a look at the other side."

Peter, surprising the rest of the group, also had a supportive comment. He said, "It was tough for me to come up with 'the other side,' but in the end, I did see some merit that I didn't see at first. I've got to give props to John here."

"Well," John smiled as he said, "thank you for the support, Peter. I'm grateful that you kept an open mind." John continued, "Okay, everyone," John said, "I think we've done a good job on building on our initial ideas. We've taken alternative views of ideas where we didn't have those views an hour or two ago. Well done."

Safe Ideation

"Let's expand our understanding of IQs by seeing how they can help us create feedback on ideas that individuals present. Remember, in this case right now, we are ultimately looking to create an *Ideal Final Result* out of all the possibilities.

"I see a set of confused faces, so let's go through this now, and, hopefully, it will become clearer. Okay?" The nods around the room were somewhat tentative, so John eased his way into the next concept. He said, "Let me explain, and I promise it will make sense. In his presentation about being the McDonald's of the cloud computing industry, Peter pointed out several aspects of McDonald's that could be important in our business:

- International brand recognition.
- Consistent product.
- Consistent customer service.
- Product is consistently safe to eat.
- Always a good cup of coffee.

"In traditional argumentation, someone else would say to Peter, 'I don't agree with your idea that international brand recognition is important to us. Let me tell you my position, and then you can have a chance to tell me yours.' What happens in this instance? Simple: Peter could get defensive, dig his feet in, and look to stay on his current path: inertia. That's not good for him, his feelings, or the overall process.

"So, I will introduce another *Innovative Question*. Let's say I don't see how international brand recognition is important to Storm's continued thriving as a company. I simply say, 'Peter, can you help me understand how international brand recognition supports Storm's excellence as a company?'" John turned to look at Peter.

Peter thought for a second, and then he said, "That's easy. The more people know about us, the more comfortable they will be with using our product. And, the more they associate us with security, the more likely they are to think of us when they are making a choice."

John replied, "That's excellent, Peter. Let me ask you, though: What did you think when I asked that question?"

Peter responded, "I didn't think about it. It was just an easy question to answer."

"Exactly!" John replied enthusiastically. "Let's continue."

"Now, let's say that I have a concern about the budget that would be involved in international brand recognition. I can ask a follow-up question and ask him, 'Peter, how would you allocate the budget dollars to make this happen?'" John looked at Peter again for an answer.

After thinking for a few seconds, Peter replied, "That's a good question. I hadn't thought about that. Can we discuss it?"

"First," John replied, "Peter, how do you feel?"

Peter replied, "What do you mean? Am I sick?"

"No," John laughed. "How do you feel about my questioning of your ideas? Good, bad, ugly?" Peter laughed back.

He replied, "I didn't even think about it. I didn't feel challenged, and I guess because I trust you, and I'm not feeling like I was in a corner, I was able to honestly answer your question."

"Yes!" Peter said.

"That's exactly it. We've created a space in which we can address concerns without attacking another and by giving each other the space to answer honestly and thoughtfully. Does that make sense to everyone?" Everyone started nodding their heads. John could see that the light bulbs had gone on.

Win-Win

"As we ask *Innovative Questions,* it's important that we remember that everyone around the table has different goals and intents," John continued. "We want to make sure that, as people talk about what they want and need, we repeatedly try to keep everyone's intents on the table. At the very least, we want to make sure, that they, at least, don't feel hurt and are part of the process." John looked around the room as he finished speaking and noticed that Devon had a scowl on his face. "Devon," John said quietly, "it looks as if something I've said has not clicked with you. Would you mind sharing what's bothering you?"

Devon replied, "I don't see how someone can have the interests of all parties in mind. I'm coming from a particular place. I need my technology to be advanced in order for the company to succeed, at least from my perspective. How can I have someone else's interest in mind?"

"Good question," John said. "So let me clarify. When you are in a discussion, there are basically three outcome combinations. Win-win; win-lose; and lose-lose. Many aspects of game theory have addressed these different permutations. When you are engaged in a business relationship, winning or losing a particular argument is not necessarily the total aim. If you are a caring human being, or even just a smart human being, you want everyone to walk away from the table feeling good about what just happened. Even when you don't care for the other people in the room, it's still important that the outcome follows a perceived fair path.

"Let me give you some background and then an example to illustrate this point. When people are going through the process of resolving a problem, there are typically four goals in operation while working through that problem: Topic, relationship, process and identity.[3]"

"The topic goal relates to the problem being solved; it is comprised of what the actual words say about what we are trying to resolve. In this case, which of our options represents our ideal goal? However, the additional goals are also important and sometimes even more important.

"Relationship goals deal specifically with how people want their relationships to be defined. For example, Peter is new to the company and would probably like to build relationships with the other people around the table. Rajesh, on the other hand, probably expects to be treated with a certain amount of deference, as he is the CEO of the company. This goal immediately translates to another one, called the identity goal, which deals with the way each of us needs to feel as an individual.

"Finally, each of us also considers the process we are going through, which means that the actual process, in our case, of making a decision, remains just as important as whether or not something is decided your way. As an example, if I spend the entire afternoon yelling at Lucy, even if we agree on the outcome, or choose the outcome she wanted, Lucy could still end up feeling quite demoralized at the end of the day."

At this point, Lucy raised her hand. "I'm confused. How can there be three other goals in addition to the outcome you are looking for? I find that contradictory."

Rajesh chimed in with, "Let me take a stab at it. Human beings, in assessing the way they are treated, aren't simply concerned about whether or not they win or lose a 'battle' of ideas. There are other aspects, including whether or not their relationship is valued by the other players in the room, which can be equally important."

---

[3] Dues, Michael. *The Art of Conflict Management: Achieving Solutions for Life, Work, and Beyond.* Chantilly, VA: The Teaching Company, 2010. Available at www.thegreat courses.com.

"Exactly," John said, "and this is critical to understanding the next aspect of win-win."

Lucy nodded her head in understanding. "I get it," she said. "That makes sense."

"Typically, we don't simply interact with people," John continued, "and then move on. We usually have a further relationship with each of them. So, each one of our interactions becomes a part of a relationship with someone, even if we don't like that person or if they don't like us. In turn, it becomes in our best interest to start thinking of what the other person needs in order to walk away from the table feeling satisfied.

"Let's explore the situation further. Devon wants to make sure that the company has the best technology possible. And, let's say he feels that McDonald's does not represent this and that having a strategic goal that says we want to be like McDonald's minimizes his important contributions to the company."

Devon chimed in, "That's interesting, John. I wouldn't have said it minimizes my contributions. You know what, though? I think it does. The McDonald's concept doesn't keep us focused on the need to be a technology innovator. And my job is to be the leader of technology innovation."

"Fair enough," John answered. "That's a very good summary of what I am trying to get at. Everyone else, what part of what Devon just said could you agree with?" There was a pause, and then John continued. "I see everyone has a confused look on their face. Remember, we can help stop our inertia by looking for common ground. Can you see any common ground here?"

Allison raised her hand and said, "Yes, we need to be a quality company."

John smiled, nodded his head, and said, "Absolutely! We've just done two things. First, we've looked at the idea from another perspective, and, perhaps more importantly, we have respected Devon by finding common ground with his idea. Excellent work!

"Let's continue. As we are trying to work through whether or not this is the best position for us to take or the best decision for us to make, effective players will take into consideration what Devon needs. Why? Because if everyone at the table feels that their needs are being met, or at least being listened to and understood, we are much more likely to have a team that is going to enthusiastically support the decision going forward. Also, since everyone at the table has an important role to play in executing the plan effectively and efficiently, we have a much better chance of achieving our stated goal when everyone's ideas and goals are considered. People work harder when their goals are involved in the outcome. In turn, this means that, by looking for everyone to win, everyone at least believes that the process considered their needs, and, in most cases, the process will address those needs in some way. Does that make sense?"

This time, as John looked around the room and at each person, starting with Lucy, he got a series of nods.

Consensus

John went on, "I want to take a moment to talk about consensus. Does consensus mean that we all talk about it and that the leader will mke a decision?"

Devon clearly had an opinion about this one, and he said, "No way! Consensus means the majority agrees."

Allison countered, "Hold on one minute. I don't agree with that, either. What if one person strongly disagrees?"

"That's a good point," John said, "and one we need to get into further. So how can we define this?"

Rajesh said, "I have a thought. Consensus means that everyone is more or less on the same page, with no one specifically disagreeing."

John smiled at Rajesh and replied, "I think that is a good start. I also think it's a bit vague and needs clarity. I would like your reaction to this thought. Consensus means that...

1. Everyone understands how and why the decision was made, and
2. Everyone commits and understands that they will execute and follow through on what's been decided,
3. Even if they argued against it in the decision-making process and even if they still disagree with it.
4. And, ultimately, whoever has the power in the room is the final decision-maker.

John wanted to drive the final point home. He said, "I want to make sure that you make peace with this last point. The person with the power is the decision-maker. If he or she has done their job right, everyone walks away from the table feeling good about the process."

John looked around the room. He could tell people were thinking about the ideas he just presented. He said, "Thoughts?"

Lucy had a question. "What if we don't have a majority, and you don't have any more time to make a final decision. How does that work out?"

"That's a great question," John said, "and it is addressed by point number 4. Ultimately, the person who has the power makes that decision. We strive to honor each of these points, and, ultimately, the person who wields the power makes the decision.

"Of course," John said, "the good part is that, by defining consensus upfront, everybody can see that there was an attempt to include them. And that makes it more likely to have consensus when everyone walks out of the meeting. Rajesh, as our fearless leader, would you like to say anything about how you will work on consensus?"

Rajesh paused for a moment and then said, "I will work like hell to have a significant majority agree. I take the responsibility of giving you the platform to state your case and listen to it with an open mind. It would be great if our decision was unanimous, and, having said that, at some point, the decision is ultimately mine, and ultimately a decision will need to be made, so I will make it. The reality of life is that I have a responsibility to the Corporation and the Board of Directors, and I take that seriously."

Honesty and Intention

"Does anyone else have any other ground rules for our *Space Creation* diagram they would like to flesh out?"

Allison started talking, "I think that it's important to come from a place of honesty. One of the things I like about working here at Storm is that we try to say what's on our mind. However, I do want to put on the table that, sometimes, my feelings do get hurt, so I think that, by considering the other process goals, I would feel better at the end of a discussion. I'd like to throw that out for consideration."

John was smiling. "Any objections from the group?"

Peter answered back, "I think that's a great idea. And I like how this group is starting to work together."

Dinner

"Okay, it's time to break for dinner," John said. "Let's take 90 minutes and meet back here for just a little bit more work." They decided as a group to cross the street to Houlihan's, a burger joint that was frequented by just about everyone in the company at least once a week. Houlihan's had only a bar and booths, so they broke up into two groups — John, Rajesh, Lucy, and Devon in one booth and then Peter and Allison in another one.

The larger group was having a lively discussion about how difficult it was to avoid the word "but." Everyone talked about how they kept either biting their tongues or cursing themselves when another team member called them on saying "but." Lucy suggested that they have a "but" jar, which was just like a swear jar, where you would have to put in a dollar each time you said "but."

In the next booth, Allison was interested in how a CIO like John had come across these theories about how to manage collaboration, conflict, and decision-making. "I mean," Allison said, "aren't CIO types typically nerds and IT geeks?"

"Well, if you are looking for the IT geek," Peter replied, "that's me. I work in the deep trenches to get the technology working. When there's a difficult problem to solve or something's broken, they call me. However, when they need someone in front of the customer, they don't call me. That's not my skill, and, honestly, I don't aspire to it."

"Okay, I get that," said Allison, "but what about John? He doesn't seem like the typical IT geek." Allison intently looked at Peter, making it clear she wanted the straight scoop.

"Well," Peter said, "John started in the trenches with me. We were both pretty technical, and, somewhere along the way, John branched out to managing people. Quite honestly, he wasn't very good at this when he first started; it didn't seem natural. He has become quite good with practice. Not only that, people respect him because they know he truly cares about them and he has their best interests at heart. He is not easy. He challenges everybody to reach their potential. And, people enjoy working with him.

"Finally, he never stops trying to get better himself. This latest stuff he's working on is the result of working with a coach. And he is not working with a coach because somebody told him he had to — he is working with a coach he met through a friend and with whom he enjoys working. So, I guess what I'm trying to say is that he is committed to getting better."

Alison looked intrigued. Her eyes told Peter that she wanted to hear more. So, Peter indulged her, "I'm not sure I buy this latest stuff, to be honest with you, and some of the stuff that John works on does seem a bit too touchy-feely for me. But — dammit, I said 'but'!" Peter smiled and emphasized the word "and." "And, in the end, it usually is quite effective. So even though I had my little outburst earlier today," Peter smiled sheepishly, "I do get what he's trying to accomplish and how he's continually trying to improve. Does that make sense?"

Allison nodded. "Okay, then, so what's your take on this *Innovative Questions* stuff?" she replied. "Do you actually think that it makes sense?"

"Well," Peter replied, "I'm waiting to hear and see more. I know I trust John, so I'm willing to give it a shot. I've been through enough situations with John to know that it's worthwhile to listen to and see where it goes. He'll also admit when something doesn't or didn't work, which I very much appreciate about him."

Just then, the waitress brought the burgers. They were big slabs of Angus beef piled high with all of the fixings. They dug in and ate their meal.

⸱ ⸱ ⸱

Picking Favorites

Back in the conference room, John got started again. "Okay folks, it's time to work on our last agenda item of the day and then get home. We have these multiple ideas, and we've taken differing viewpoints to work on these ideas from other perspectives. It's time to narrow them down. Just before we got back, I posted each of the ideas on the walls around the room. I've also given each of you a red stack of Post-it notes and a green stack of Post-it notes. I want each of you to walk around the room to each of the ideas and put a red Post-it note where you don't like the idea and a green Post-it note where you do. Let's see how many viable options come out of this process. Sound okay?"

These instructions were easily swallowed by the group, and in their late-in-the-day stupor, everyone just quietly nodded their heads. "Okay," said John, "let's get cracking." Each of the team members walked around and placed their notes as they wanted. In the end, everyone took their seats again, and John looked around the room.

"Well," John said, "it looks like we have three clear winners. That's good; it will make this task easier." As he said this, he took down the losing ideas and continued, "Now, I'm going to clear up the Post-it notes," he said as he walked around taking off the Post-it notes and putting them back on the table. "I'd like you now to pick your favorites. The one you want to be the outcome. And, if you have two favorites and can't decide which one you like better, that will be fine with me. But if you can narrow your choice down to one, that would be better. Questions?"

Allison raised her hand, "Is this the best way to make a decision? I mean, isn't this just like Democratic voting? Could we be missing something good?"

John replied, "That's a good point, Allison. I like the way you're thinking. Let me ask the group a question: Does anyone feel that one of these ideas we've removed has merit and should remain?"

Peter raised his hand. "You know, while I don't like the McDonald's idea as a whole, I would like to take some of the ideas we talked about — is that okay?"

Lucy chimed in as well, "I agree. Can we just leave that up as an additional reference while we fine tune?"

John was smiling. "I'm impressed with how you guys are working together. Let's absolutely do that. Now, let's go around and see who has favorites on the wall." When they were done, it became clear that there were two favorites:

1. Bring great value and security to our cloud customers.
2. Change the computing paradigm for individual businesses by providing exceptional service and products one client at a time.

Having learned from the previous comment, John started with, "By leaving out the third option, does anyone feel we are missing something?"

Allison responded, "I have two thoughts. First, I'd like to leave up all of the ideas so that we can refer to them. That way, we will, hopefully, not miss anything. Also, I think we can do better on the wording on both of these. Do you think that we could collaborate a bit more and make these better before we decide which one to pick?"

John replied, "I think those are both fantastic ideas. Any objections?" John looked around the room to enthusiastic smiles. He continued, "Great. I will put the other ideas back up, and let's break into groups and take the rest of our time to work out a better *Ideal Final Result*. We'll meet again here first thing in the morning. *And*, you can take this opportunity to incorporate any other ideas from the documents that we are not using. Sound okay?" John got nods around the room, and they broke up into groups to fine-tune the two ideas.

◼ ◼ ◼

Breakfast Debrief

The next morning at breakfast, Rajesh was seated at the kitchen table with his wife Linda and his two kids, TJ and Sarah. Linda was 5 foot 4, a brunette with wavy hair cut shoulder length, and had met Rajesh while in college at UCLA. She immediately fell for his sense of humor and his amazing intellect. TJ was 12 years old, while Sarah was 16. TJ loved every aspect of every sport, and Sarah was girl through and through, and, although academically quite smart, she had no interest in either dating boys or driving cars.

As part of a family tradition, they went around the breakfast table starting with the youngest, sharing with the family the best thing that had happened the day before. TJ started and talked about how he had had a fantastic soccer practice and scored four goals in his scrimmage. Sarah talked about the blog post she just finished late last night on too much materialism in the world. Since Rajesh was two years younger than his wife, having skipped 7th and 11th grades, he always got to go before her. "I have to tell you, our new CIO started this week, John Adamson, and he is not your typical CIO. You may remember that he is a good friend of mine from college. Anyway, he's helping us work on what he calls an *Ideal Final Result* for our company strategy, and, I have to say I'm enjoying it."

Sarah looked interested and asked, "What was so great about it? I mean, isn't he just a technology weenie?" Rajesh smiled as he responded, "You know, I thought he was just a great technology guy, but he's so much more. It goes to show that even people who weren't previously good with others can improve by listening to advice and then acting on it. Today, we were able to work through conflict in the most effective way I've ever seen. It's almost like we have a magic wand to open up this space for people to truly work together well. It's amazing."

■   ■   ■

Picking the Ideal Final Result

Later that morning, the group met back in the conference room. John asked each group to talk about their idea for two minutes or less. Allison got up first. "Storm Technologies is dedicated to bringing exceptional value, reasonably well secured, for every interaction our clients have with our company and our technology. To us, this means that every product brings good value to the client, has good security, and our clients are always happy."

Peter raised his hand. "I have a question."

Allison started to reply, but John interrupted. "Let's save our questions for after we hear from our second group. Okay? Now, for simplicity's sake, let's call this the 'Value Added Model.' Good job, Allison. Who's up with the second idea?"

Devon got up and started to talk, "Storm Technologies wants to raise the bar in everything we do. We will not settle for second best in any area and we will always be the industry leader in technology and security. So, our *Ideal Final Result* is: Computing Paradigm version 2.0: the very best in products and security coupled with exceptional service, one client at a time. We believe that in order to compete with large-scale vendors, we have to have the very best product both technologically and security-wise every time."

"Okay," said John, "let's call this one the 'Best-of-Breed Model.' Let me ask each group a question. If anyone on either team could switch sides to supporting the other idea, would you do it now?" Nobody wanted to switch. Each team member wanted to stick with the idea that they had spent several hours on the day before. "Fair enough," John said, "we've made our opening arguments. I'm assuming that, because no one wants to switch, we are now ready to identify our best *Ideal Final Result*. Sound fair?" John got three smiles and nods and two skeptical looks from Allison and Peter.

Even though he could see he had some ground left to cover, he thought that the situation was good enough to get underway. He dove right in. "Before I move on to our next set of *Innovative Questions*, I want to give you a bit of background on how to select the right *Innovative Question* in each situation."

"Remember, *Innovative Questions* allow for the creation of *Safe Space* so we can work through conflict and decision-making effectively. In traditional argumentation, collaborative conflict is used to point out flaws in each other's arguments. While, historically, many have found this method effective in getting to a result, so much of human nature gets in the way that a lot is lost in the argumentation process. That said, there are a number of elements in the classical argumentation process that are critically important to facilitating *Innovative Questions*. So, I'm going to take a little time to talk about the elements of argumentation so you can use that to formulate appropriate *Innovative Questions*.

> The authors are deeply indebted to three series of lectures from the Great Courses for helping us explain the foundation of *Space Creation* and *Innovative Questions*. All of these courses are available at http://www.thegreatcourses.com/ and are referenced separately in the text.

"In order for an argument to exist at all, there must be three elements. First, there must be a disagreement. Clearly, we have two worthy ideas on the table, and some of you prefer one of the ideas, and some of you prefer the other for various reasons, including cognitive biases and your personal preferences. For my point, yes, we have a disagreement on the outcome.

"Second, the disagreement must matter. If you do not feel passionate or care about the outcome, then there is no point in going through the argument. If Devon, for example, did not feel strongly about having the very best in technology, then he might as well just sit down and go with the 'Value Added' model, because it's just not important to him. This is very similar to one spouse saying to the other that their choice of where they go to dinner is just fine with them. Why waste the effort if it doesn't matter? Does that make sense?"

Lucy raised her hand. "Okay, I think I'm missing something here. Even if I think that the 'Value Added' idea is a tiny bit better than the

'Only the Very Best' idea, should I still make the argument? I mean, what if it's just a minor difference?"

John answered her, "Excellent question. The answer is, 'It depends.' If you could go either way, then it's not worth a lot of energy. Why? First, you have to spend time having the argument. Second, if someone else feels strongly about an idea, and you don't, why not let them run with it? We all like expressing our passion. And if it's about the same to you, why not let it go for the other person? Is that a reasonable explanation, Lucy?" Lucy nodded.

"Okay, so I'll continue." John said. "The third point is 'the desire to result in agreement.' What does that mean? It means that, through having the argument, we have to have a desire to come to some sort of agreement. If I'm a Democrat and you are a Republican, and we know we are not going to change the other person's mind, or at least maybe I know I'm not going to change my mind, why argue? It's just going to be aggravating, so...." John sort of knew this was coming, so he was ready for the interruption from Peter.

"Now hold on, just wait a minute now. Let me give you my scenario. Okay, I'm the technical guy. I know whether or not technology works. So, someone comes in from marketing —no offense, Allison —with a 'great' idea. She says she wants to market a computer that has, say, a long-distance keyboard which uses a new technology she found from a vendor that lets that person walk around up to 2000 feet away from the computer and receive simple text messages on the keyboard. Now, after my review, it is clear that the solution is not secure and subject to repeated failure. This marketing person, not Allison," Peter smiled, "doesn't get it at all and argues with me. In my mind, there is no argument. The technology is not a good technology. Period. So, why have the argument?"

John paused for a minute to think about it. "Peter, is it possible that you aren't right? I mean, could the marketing person be right?" Peter looked dumbfounded. So, John rephrased the question, "Peter, let's practice another *Innovative Question*. If you could wave a magic wand and fix all the problems, what would you do?"

Peter responded, "Well, I would start all over."

John replied, "Well, is it possible that it could be fixed?"

"Of course, it's possible," Peter answered, "But you and I both know that that's not the case. This is just a stupid technology. So there is no argument."

From looking around the room, you could tell that everyone thought that John seemed stuck. But John wasn't going to lose ground with his progress on his point just yet. He knew he could work with Peter and turn around the conversation. John said, "Peter, you brought up an interesting point, which brings me to the next few elements of argumentation. So, let me answer your question by showing you a little bit more of the argumentation roadmap.

"First, let's take a look at a drawing that shows how an effective argument is structured.

Basic Argument Structure

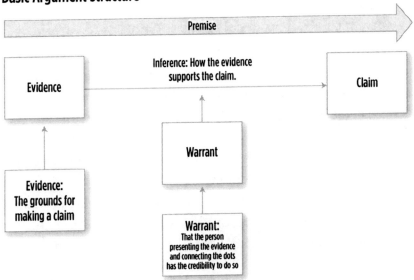

Figure 5.2

"This diagram is called a basic argument structure. I've adapted it from a lecture by Professor David Zarefsky from Northwestern University.[4] Here's how it works. When we want to make a point, we are trying to establish a 'claim,' in classical argumentation terms. We want that claim to be understood and accepted by the person or persons to whom we are making the argument. As we talked about a few minutes ago, if the person we are talking to accepts the claim, there is no argument. Claim accepted, no issue. On the other hand, if the person does not accept the claim, we need to present evidence to support the claim. Does everyone get that concept?

"Okay, great." John continued in response to nods. "In order to present evidence to support a claim, we must make an inference. An inference is the way we connect the dots between the evidence and the claim. Can we all agree on that concept?"

Rajesh nodded his head. "Of course, that's basic logic; we present evidence in order to make our point, or 'claim,' as you are calling it here. That's pretty simple."

"Right," John said. "Even though this is a simple concept, it's important because understanding this basic part of argumentation and how we connect the dots helps us as we sort through a disagreement. Let's take a look at the disagreement that Peter is talking about. Peter's claim alleges that the keyboard/texting technology is unusable. The evidence he presents shows that it will periodically fail from time to time and that it is not secure, therefore subjecting the computer to some sort of compromise. Peter, is that accurate?"

"Yes," Peter replied, "absolutely. Thank you for checking with me."

Allison decided to join in the fray. After all, it was a marketing person who was being attacked. She said, "So, who died and made Peter

---

[4]   Zarefsky, David. *Argumentation: The Study of Effective Reasoning, 2nd Edition.* Chantilly, VA: The Teaching Company, 2005, page 21 of the accompanying pdf. Available at www.thegreatcourses.com.

the expert on whether or not this is an essential problem with using the technology? Maybe it's not important. So what do you do then?"

"Well," John said, "that's the next part. We call this the 'warrant.' The warrant is what gives us the authority to make the claim that we are making, based upon the evidence that we are presenting. In this case, Peter is the computer expert. He understands things like reliability and security."

"Yeah, so?" countered Allison. "And I'm the marketing expert, and I understand things like getting things to market and how a lot of users won't care about security or whether or not the keyboard periodically fails. They will just think about the brand that brought the keyboard to market, what a great technology it is, and what a great company we must be. So what happens to Peter's 'warrant' now?" As she said this last sentence, Allison rolled her eyes.

"Well, that's an excellent question, although I have to say that eye rolling is most certainly not a part of *Innovative Questions.*" John smiled.

In response, Allison blushed and said, "Point well made, I apologize." John continued, "I think this poses a good opportunity for us to explore argumentation a bit further. First, let me introduce another concept. It's called 'premise.' A premise represents the set of assumptions that you are bringing to the end claim. So, Peter has presented a premise that security and reliability are key to a product's success. And that makes sense from his perspective. If his systems go down or someone steals data off of them, he is going to be called on the carpet.

"Now, on the other hand, if Allison can't sell a sufficient quantity of product to keep her company in business, she's got a problem. From her premise, sales and market share are critically important. Getting customers is important. She has a similarly valid but different 'inference' and a similarly valid but different premise."

Rajesh raised his hand. "John, all of this is very interesting," Rajesh started to say but, and stopped himself. He paused and continued, "How do we get past this problem? We seem to be stuck."

John's eyes lit up. "Exactly," he said as he smiled broadly. "We have reached a point of *Stasis*. We are stuck. And, classical argumentation has a lot to say about this. Let me talk about this for just a little bit, and I think you will see why it's helpful that we understand how an argument is made up."

Topoi

"Before we talk about where we are stuck, we have to talk about where we are. This is the concept of *Topoi*, or places. This is another way in which we can dissect any disagreement. In argumentation, each claim can be one of four different types of things. It can be a fact, a definition, a value, or policy. Let me explain each of these in a way that's clearer than just listing them out.

"A fact is something that everyone should be able to agree on. If the keyboard we are arguing about is dropped on the floor and breaks in half, the keyboard is broken. There is no dispute about this, just like we would not argue about whether or not it is 55° outside. The thermometer says 55°; it's 55°.

"Now, let me say just a quick thing about facts. Sometimes, what is accepted as a fact isn't a fact. For example, for hundreds of years, the vast majority of people thought that the earth was the center of the universe. They didn't understand gravity, so when things fell back towards the earth, it could only be because the Earth was at the center. Galileo was a great example of someone who suffered from knowing a different truth than what was accepted. I'm not saying there is much to do about this right now. I just think it's important that we be aware of the fact (that's kind of a double use of the word) that facts are not always set in stone. For example, in today's world, we hear differing facts about global warming from seeming experts. And, recently there has also been a challenge to Einstein's "speed of light" theory.[5] So facts can actually change.

"How do we assess whether or not the keyboard is broken as a matter of a fact? In this case, the classical criterion is whether or not the keyboard is usable for what you bought it to do. The criterion is satisfied because we can no longer use the keyboard, as it is broken into two pieces, does not turn on, and won't type to the computer.

"Okay, let's move on to the definition *Topoi*. A definition is harder. For example, the definition of whether or not this keyboard is usable. Peter says it's not. Allison says it is. In Peter's mind, 'usable' means it will work all the time and it will be secure. In Allison's mind, 'usable' means someone will be happy if they buy it. Allison believes that her users understand that there are quirks in new products, and they can get over those.

"In both cases, meaning Peter's and Allison's, the interpretation by classical standards can be proved as both relevant and fair. The technology person says it's not a workable solution; the marketing person, speaking on behalf of the masses, says that it is. How do we choose?

"One answer could be that whoever has the power gets to choose. Certainly, that's one way for the decision to be made. What if, say, Rajesh couldn't decide. He respects both Peter and Allison, and he didn't know which one had the stronger case. What criteria would he use to decide? What questions would he ask to get to the best result on this particular issue? Any ideas?"

Devon raised his hand. "I do. You could ask for case studies and marketing research. The person with the best evidence should win the point."

---

5   http://www.washingtonpost.com/opinions/gone-in-60-nanoseconds/2011/10/06/gIQAf1RERL_story.html.

Allison was nodding and said, "That's an excellent point. I could do focus groups, for example."

John responded with, "Excellent points, everyone. You could present more evidence in each case, and knowing that you are here helped you decide the next question to ask. Let me continue then.

"A value is even harder still. A value is something like saying murder is wrong. Most people agree that murder is wrong, but what about capital punishment? In this case, we can see how *Topoi* can be valuable. Knowing that we are discussing a value, let's us delve deeper into the claim that is being made. This brings us to the same diagram that we looked at when we started this discussion of argumentation. What's the evidence? Can you present evidence that makes your case, do you have a warrant to do so, and does it resonate with the audience? The more compelling argument should win the case. Luckily, because values can be a sticky area, we're not dealing with values today, at least not yet.

"Finally, policy deals with the way government and institutions set policies. It's complicated because whether or not a policy is valid can get pretty intense. Let's skip over this for our discussion today. I know that was a lot of material all at once. Any questions?"

Rajesh raised his hand. "Okay, I have to say, I think you've lost me. My brain is spinning."

John smiled and replied, "Just bear with me a little bit more. I'm going to put all of this together right now. Okay?" Rajesh took a deep breath and nodded. John went back to his monologue, "Once we understand these four levels of *Topoi*, or at least the three out of four (fact, definition, value) that we will be dealing with mostly, and the other elements of argumentation I've just outlined, we can move on to the critical concept of where we are stuck, or *Stasis*. And that, my friends, allows us to competently and successfully get unstuck and move on.

Stasis

"*Stasis* helps us understand how we will get over differences and find common ground. We will be using common ground often as a tool as we are trying to figure out the best of the two vision statements. Okay, let's jump in. There are four classical definitions of *Stasis* — conjecture: whether or not the actual act occurred; definition: the definition for an act; quality: whether the act is justified; and place: whether the conversation is occurring in the proper place or forum."

Lucy chimed in, "John, I have to say, you have me more than puzzled. I am not following you at all. In fact, you are making my head hurt a little bit."

"Well," John replied, "Lucy, and everyone else, you have a good point. I'm going too fast, so let me slow down. I'm sorry; sometimes I get excited about this stuff." John took a deep breath. "Let me come at this from the beginning, and then we can take a break. *Stasis* provides us with some shortcuts that help us figure out how to best ask *Innovative Questions* about an argument and move through each conflict on the way to determining or getting to the *Ideal Final Result*."

Everyone still had that deer-in-headlights look, so John paused and continued more slowly, "Let's start out with something we talked about earlier on. Let me pose the following question: Are our primary competitors Amazon and Google actually stealing accounts from us? Are we actually losing accounts to them now that we would have previously won?"

Allison stood up. She couldn't contain herself. "Come on, John — let's be real. We are obviously losing those accounts."

"Okay," John said. "First, let me point out that this is a *Stasis* of conjecture: Is the disagreement centering around whether or not something occurred. Make sense?" To looks of understanding around the room, John asked the following question, "Does everyone agree with Allison's point?" Devon and Rajesh, the existing team representatives, both nodded their heads. Well then, we have a situation where we have stipulated the answer. On the other hand, if we didn't all agree, like on the keyboard issue, we would identify that we were stuck in conjecture, and could ask certain types of questions to get unstuck, and thereby get closer to resolution. Just before, for example, Allison and Peter presented two sides of an argument to this imaginary keyboard. Where are we stuck? We are stuck at the definition of whether or not the keyboard was salable and workable. Does that make sense?"

Devon's hand shot up. "Dude, I have to say that I'm still confused. Can you help me out?"

John put up his hands in a conciliatory gesture. "Okay, let me explain a bit more with another example.

"The *Stasis* of definition, the second *Stasis* point, centers around the how we define something. In our exercise of defining our goals, in our *Ideal Final Result,* we have created two definitions of achieving where we want to end up: 'Value add' and 'best-of-breed.' Clearly, some controversy exists in this group as to the definition of 'value add.' Is the definition 'as good as you can get for a certain price'? Is the definition 'the best value for a customer,' or is the definition 'the very best we can give the customer'? These are all viable options. Figuring out that we are stuck here helps us understand what to do and which *Innovative Question* or *Questions* we should ask to get unstuck and move on to the *Ideal Final Result.* "Devon, am I making some more sense?"

"Yes," Devon replied, "you are. So, while I might think the definition of 'value add' means the very best available security to protect our customers, Allison might think that it means innovative enough to get someone to buy it. Right?"

"Yes," John replied, "exactly! And now, once we know where we are stuck, we can ask questions. Like, 'Allison, how would you prove that your customers will buy something that is innovative and that has quirks?' Does this make sense, everyone?"

As the light bulb started to go on in the heads around the room over the course of the next 10 seconds, John smiled and said, "Whew! I was starting to sweat there for a minute. Notice that I didn't tell Allison she was wrong. I asked her how she was going to prove her point. The way the *Space Creation* process works, you either resolve each issue as you get stuck, or you break down the issue into other smaller issues that can more easily be resolved."

John took a deep breath and said, "Now that I've gotten everyone over that hump, let me make sure I'm being complete in discussing *Stasis*. The next *Stasis* point is quality. Quality is a value judgment. It's whether something is right or wrong. For example, you might argue that it's wrong to not give your customers the very best security that you possibly can because you didn't want to spend the research and development dollars to get there. Make sense?" Nods around the room. "Once you know that you are stuck here, you can focus your questions on the quality until you get unstuck.

"Let me finish up with the place *Stasis*, which isn't as relevant here, but it's good to know in general," John continued, "The *Stasis* of place asks whether or not an issue is being addressed in the appropriate place or forum. And, if this is where we are stuck, we can find out where we agree and where we disagree.

"I can see I've just thrown a lot at you. It was important to get through that, and I'm glad we are done. Any questions?"

Peter raised his hand. "Are you saying there's only one point in the entire argument where we could be stuck? That seems a bit simplistic to me."

John replied, "Absolutely not. An argument could go through many, many *Stasis* points. The idea is that, at each place where we are stuck, we identify the sticking point, and we work to overcome it. And, if the sticking point is too big, we break it down into smaller sticking points. Is everyone okay with that idea?" More nods around the room "So here's the cornerstone concept for me behind *Stasis* — once you have identified where you are stuck, you can ask appropriate questions and much more quickly get to a win-win solution. And, that is why we study all this ancient stuff."

"I can see that everyone's getting tired, so let's take lunch."

Before they broke, Rajesh spoke up. "Listen, John, I see where you're going. Just keep in mind we need to be finished by tomorrow. We need to get out our new set of marketing materials, and they are due by next Friday, so we have a limited amount of time that we can work on this before we have to finish up those documents."

John paused for a minute, as if he hadn't carefully thought this through. "Okay, how about this? Can we work a little bit late into the evening so we at least get through our first round? I promise we'll wrap up this session by 8 PM tonight. Then we can finish up tomorrow." John got a set of nods, although they weren't all that enthusiastic.

■ ■ ■

Practicing Innovative Questions

After lunch, they reconvened in the conference room. Everyone looked a little bit tired, so John decided to take a different tack. "Okay, I can see you are all getting a bit tired of listening to me talk. Let's have a little bit of practice. Sound okay?"

Peter answered for the group. "Now you're talking. Let's get down to work on picking our *Ideal Final Result*. Since Devon and I are on the same team and we talked about it at lunch, we are ready to go first." John nodded assent. He motioned with his hands for them to start talking.

Devon started in. "As you all know, our idea is all about excellence. We think it's pretty clear why you should choose excellence over value, but we wanted to give you a few reasons. First, we believe there is no merit to the claim that people will choose value over high quality. In our opinion, we believe they will always pick high quality. We also don't believe there is sufficient expertise in the room or appropriate evidence to counter our claim. And finally, in this context of hack after hack on people's systems being reported in the news day after day, we need to be secure."

John stood up. He said, "Devon, your points are excellent and very strong. And, I'd like to help you modify them so that they allow for *Space Creation*. Let me make a point first. Allison, how did hearing what Devon had to say make you feel?"

Allison responded with, "I'm not feeling too great about this process and Devon right now. I take a lot of pride in my work, and I want to be seen as someone who is a contributor to the team. This did not make me feel that way."

Devon responded right away. "Allison, I'm truly sorry. That's absolutely not my intention." Allison smiled and nodded, and John chimed in, "That's exactly my point. Directly making arguments at each other hits emotional buttons and can do damage to relationships. Remember our four process goals? Well, some of those got stomped on here.

"Let me show you a better way. I'm going to re-create one of Devon's arguments with an *Innovative Question*. On the first point, that there is no merit to the argument that people will choose value over high quality, I would instead propose that we use the question. Allison, can you help me understand why you think people will choose value over high quality? Allison, how does that question make you feel?"

Allison smiled and responded right away, "I like that question. It lets me make my point."

Devon had a point to make and raised his hand, "John, I have a question: How do I get my point across that I disagree?"

John replied right away with a big smile on his face, "Well, let's look at the principles that we've been discussing. First, start with common ground. You can try using the statement, 'Allison, I agree that providing value is important, and I'd also like to see strong security in the equation. Do you have any ideas how we can incorporate that?'"

John looked around the room to see that everyone was following him, and it seemed that they were. He continued, "What did I do here? I used 'and' to show that I was building on her idea, and I told her what my concerns were. I asked her, respecting her identity, our relationship, and the overall process, if she could help me work on my goal. As I knew exactly where I was stuck, what our *Stasis* was, I was able to ask an effective question. Everyone okay with where we have been so far?" John could see smiles and nods around the room.

"Let me just take a slight detour here to warn the group about a habit I used to have that I've been working on — needing to win. Getting to the best outcome means we need to leave our need to win behind. The only winning that should be going on is by the entire team. Are you okay with that, Allison?"

"I definitely have an issue with needing to win," Allison said, "so I see what you're saying. That doesn't mean I still don't want to win, just that I'm going to have to adjust the way I win and how I define winning."

John continued, "Good, Allison — thanks for your willingness to be open. Okay," John took a breath as he got back on track, "I know Allison's group did some work on their presentation earlier, and I would like for them to take some time to revise their arguments using what we just learned about *Innovative Questions*. Sound okay?"

▪   ▪   ▪

Arguments Revised with *Innovative Questions*

Allison was ready when they reconvened a few minutes later. "The reason that lowest common denominator firms like McDonald's are so successful is that not everyone has enough money to buy the best of the best, and what they are actually looking for is good value. In each of our neighborhoods, we always know about that one restaurant where the value is great and the food is great, and it's not fancy. That restaurant is always busy."

"We want Storm Technologies to always be successful and profitable. And, we also recognize that the majority of the population is neither searching for the Cadillac solution nor can they afford it. The battle between Microsoft versus Apple (before Apple's resurgence) years ago proved that. The key concept to consider is: How good is good enough? Also, there are a number of elements that come along with being the value leader. For us, this does not mean that we are the low-cost leader. We will continue to provide top-flight security to the market. With that goal in mind, the effort to remain the very best can hurt our ability to spend money on marketing and sales efforts, and so we would like to propose a balanced approach.

"According to a well-known concept referred to as the Pareto analysis, it takes approximately 80% of the effort to do the last 20% of the work. While we are the best of the breed right now, I believe we now need to focus on building our market share and name brand recognition. For example, when I hold up this child's toy with this golden arches logo, everyone knows what it stands for — McDonald's. We are not saying that we shouldn't focus on bringing excellent products to market. I'm saying that, strategically, we have to balance all of the elements of business for a successful outcome.

"As a case study, I'd like to talk about a company called Rackspace. While they are highly successful, they have continued to be a niche player, because they focus only on the high end, whereas, on the other hand, a company like Go Daddy has become wildly successful by being the value leader. They are not the lowest-priced provider in the market. They provide a good product with reasonable security. So, that's why we re-present to you the tagline:

"Storm Technologies is dedicated to bringing exceptional value, well secured, for every interaction our clients have with our company and our technology. To us, this means that every product brings the customer a desired value, including security, and we have happy customers who value our product and service very highly and continue to do business with us."

With that, Allison finished. The group could see that Peter was all ready to jump all over her argument. Knowing the ground rules, he took a deep breath, stood up, and started to talk about his group's idea:

"Okay, I'm going to try John's method." Peter took a deep breath. "Company after company has failed because they became complacent and did not invest sufficient dollars into research and development to stay best-of-breed." Peter took a quick glance at John to see how he was doing, and in response John put his hand up in a stopping motion. "Peter, can I make a suggestion?" To Peter's nod, John said, "Can you ask Allison to help you understand something?"

"Ah," Peter replied, "I get it. Let me rephrase my question with another example. Both Kodak and Polaroid were the strongest in their particular market. Kodak, for example, owned a vast majority of the market share in film sales. Polaroid owned almost the entire market in instant photography. Both of those companies did not sufficiently manage their transition to the digital model, partly because they were stuck in their current paradigm, and partly because they did not change. Both companies are shadows of their former selves. Allison, how would you address this type of situation in your model?"

Allison smiled. "Excellent question. I'm not proposing that we don't spend any money on research and development. I'm just proposing that we balance our spend between R&D, value proposition, and marketing. I would always include our entire management team as we charted our course, so we could have a balanced outcome."

John was smiling. He said to Allison, "How did that question feel?" Allison smiled back. "That felt pretty good. I felt like I could collaboratively and safely respond." "Excellent," John said, "and, Peter, great job on reworking your question. Does everyone see how you can change the modality and create space?" John got nods all around. "Who else would like a shot at forming an *Innovative Question?*"

Peter was smiling as he got up to talk. At the same time he got up, Lucy got up, too. She said, "I think I'd like to take a shot." Peter realized he had been dominating the conversation a bit too long, so he said as he sat down, bowing slightly toward Lucy, "No problem. I gladly defer to you."

Lucy started, "I understand the idea of the McDonald's model, *and* I don't think we have enough definition to understand what 'value-added' means." John smiled and interrupted Lucy. "Lucy, I like how you used *and*. Can I please rephrase that question just a little bit?" Lucy smiled and said 'Yes' to John. "I also like what you did with finding common ground. I would strengthen that just a little bit. Let's try this one on for size. How does, 'I can see where there is a lot of merit in your value-added model. Can you define the specific elements of how the model works a bit more for me?' Lucy, how does that feel to you?"

Lucy answered, "Wow, a small change of words makes it feels a lot nicer."

"Exactly," John replied. "You made Allison feel good by agreeing with something, and then you asked for a bit of clarification. And, to be crystal clear, I am not advocating falsely agreeing. I am advocating that you look for where you do agree. Finally, remember, words have meanings, and it takes only one skillful participant in the conversation to make a world of difference."

"Can I try it again?" Lucy asked, and, in response to a nod, she said, "I feel that the last point Allison made, about balancing excellence and value is a solid point. But," Lucy made a face, "dammit, I said 'but!'" Lucy paused, took a breath, and said, with emphasis, "*And,* I find it somewhat at odds — no, that's not right. Let me try it again. I'd like to understand how balancing excellence and value works. Can you explain it some more to me, Allison?" John responded with an emphatic, "Yes! Well done. Let's take a quick break and then reconvene."

Fine Tuning Arguments

When the group returned, John jumped right in. "I'd like to talk about a couple of other strategies that help you fine-tune your *Innovative Questions.* First, I believe that you should always check in with the other person or people in the room as you are going back and forth through the elements of a discussion. As an example, I always suggest that, after making a statement, you ask the other person, "Would you agree with that?' Their answer will steer the dialogue and let you know where you stand.

"Now, here's a point of clarification on agreement versus understanding: Remember, someone can say that they understand. That does not mean that they agree with you. A follow-on question could be, 'I know you understand. Do you agree?'

"I want to remind you that this is not about winning — it's about finding the best solution while building on teamwork and synergy. If we can identify flaws in an argument in *a Safe Space,* we can make it better, whether the flaw is our own or someone else's. The key here is intent: Does everyone in the group see everyone else as truly trying to come to the best decision, or are some people trying to win for themselves? Is everyone on board with that concept?

"So," John continued after receiving nods from the group, "I have a challenge for everyone. Now that you know a little bit more about

Innovative Questions, what types of questions could we ask to create our *Ideal Final Result?*"

Peter raised his hand and John nodded at him. "Okay," Peter started, "what are we trying to achieve?"

"Great start," John said. "What other questions might be asked?" The group went around the table, throwing out a number of different suggestions:

- How can we get there?
- What could we do differently?
- Is there anything we could do more of or start?
- Is there anything we are doing right now that we should stop?
- What are we doing well right now?
- How can we work better together?

They went on for a few minutes, and then John stopped the dialogue. "Okay," he said. "First, I want to propose two questions that I think you will find useful when in the middle of solving a problem. The first one, which I introduced earlier, is, 'Is it possible that the opposite of what you are saying is true?' There is, I want to point out, a flaw with the 'opposite' question. And, that is that not everyone has the mental prowess or creativity to put their mind around that question. At least not right away. So there's another question that is a good stepping stone to the opposite question." John paused and continued, "'If you could wave a magic wand and make this work exactly how you wanted it to, what would you do?' I have a number of variations on this one, and as you can see, this one is a lot easier to grasp. Does everyone get that one?"

This time, Peter started in. "I do want to say that, when I first heard John talk about these two questions, I thought he was full of crap. I suggest giving him a minute to show you how well they work."

John smiled and continued, "Thanks Peter — that means a lot to me. Let's continue with some more practice."

Devon raised his hand. "I'm going to say I'm a little bit skeptical right now. I'm not sure that there is a difference between a question focused on showing someone to be wrong or simply making the statement."

"Ah," John countered, "that's where I hope to prove you wrong. The way we string words together along with their meanings has monumental impact. Can you stick with me for a few more minutes?"

In response to getting a nod from Devon, John said, "Let's get started with some questions. Any takers?"

After no one else volunteered, Rajesh said, "I'm going to give this a shot, and I have to admit I feel a little bit silly." Rajesh was smiling as he asked the question: "Allison, is it possible that the opposite of your McDonald's statement is true? That only being best-of-breed could be a viable option?"

Allison was looking at Rajesh for a few seconds. She seemed to be deeply pondering the question. "Okay, let's talk this out." She spoke the following question very slowly, "Could best-of-breed be a viable option without the other elements? You know what, I can play that game as well. Let's make both sides work. Devon, how do you see best-of-breed working without being a value-added solution, without sales and marketing, and without exceptional customer service?"

Devon was smiling as he responded, "You know, I already see the power of the questions. It's interesting, I can see now that I wasn't fully thinking the solution through. I never thought about the need for customer service; I was focused on making sure we had best-of-breed product. So, in John's language, I think we actually have more common ground than we think."

Devon continued, "I'd like to think that we can find a balance between aggressively putting as much money into research and development as we can while still maintaining excellence in marketing, sales, and customer service. John, I have to say, I'm getting it now. What a great alternative to a knockdown, drag-out fight!"

At this point, Allison chimed in as well, "And, I have to say, I think I was underestimating the value-added benefit. I like what you just said a lot. I think it's a good starting point for getting to our *Ideal Final Result.*"

John stepped in at this point. He said "ladies and gentlemen, I actually think that we are almost there. It's getting late, so let's reconvene in the morning with fresh minds and do some wordsmithing."

▪   ▪   ▪

Ideal Final Result

The next morning, the group reconvened in the conference room. Everyone was buzzing with energy. John said to them, "What pieces from the two statements *can we put together that work as our Ideal Final Result?*"

Allison jumped in. "I think Devon had it exactly right yesterday. I think that, when we swapped perspectives, we found the common ground. Here's what I would propose, as I scribbled out last night: 'Storm Technologies commits to being an exceptional value to its clients. We commit to working toward a balance of best-of-breed technology and research & development supported by brand recognition and world-class sales and marketing efforts. All of this will be delivered to our users via fantastic customer service.'"

As John looked around the room, he could see that everyone was digesting what Allison had said and was mapping it to their internal vision of what they had discussed. One by one, they started to nod and smile. Rajesh jumped in to sum it up. "I think I see what happened here. Remarkable. We have honored the four goals of outcome, so everyone agrees because everyone has a piece of the answer. We got to this place by identifying the *Stasis* point so we could get past it. And, we did it respectfully and skillfully by creating *Safe Space.*"

▨   ▨   ▨

The Final Question

Later that night, Rajesh was at the table with his family. It was his turn to talk, and he just couldn't wait. "I am absolutely amazed at the power of these two questions that John, our new CIO, taught us. It took us some time to understand exactly where our contention points were, and, when we finally got there, I got the first glimpse of what was going on.

"You know, I never thought about how upset people can get when they directly receive criticism about their ideas. This one question that John asked changed the whole game. Not only did we get a great result, people were working together instead of just defending their point of views and feeling attacked.

"Okay, to be honest, there were two questions, but we needed only one of them to turn it around."

Rajesh's daughter Sarah was looking particularly interested. "Well," she said, "when are you going to tell us the question?"

Rajesh laughed. "The question is, 'Could the opposite of what you are saying be true?'" As he anticipated, his family looked at him with a blank stare. "Think about it," he said, "turn around your thinking and try to take the other side."

"You mean," Sarah said, "that when I was at the mall with Debbie today and she told me that the dress I tried on looked horrible and I was angry at her, I could have tried for a minute to think that it might have looked horrible on me?"

"Absolutely," Rajesh said, "is that something you think you could do?"

"Well," Sarah said, "it depends. I guess if I got a couple of seconds to think about it by being asked this question, I might have been able to stop and think rationally instead of reacting emotionally. Why don't you try it on me the next time we have an argument and we can see how it works out?" The whole family laughed.

■   ■   ■

Back to Innovative Questions

The Storm fable shows that *Innovative Questions* allow us to create space for solving difficult problems and work toward better outcomes. Remember, we have defined *Space Creation* to show that multiple foundational elements must be in place in order to most effectively come up with a decision, the *Ideal Final Result*. We build this foundation through our actions and through the words that help define those actions.

The fable shows how changing around the words you use and how you use them helps us arrive at a positive outcome. Furthermore, we show that it's important to understand the four goals of outcome: Topic, identity, relationship, and process. Because human beings are more than just black-and-white, because they are emotional creatures, the entire practice of *Innovative Questions* is built upon Cicero's "bedrock of principles" concept. The process does not work without a moral element.

Where Are We?

In the fable, we also explored how understanding some basic elements of argumentation and the concept of *Stasis* allows for us to ask questions about where we are, and, more importantly where are we stuck. Once we understand these seemingly simple points, we can formulate *Innovative Questions* to help us get past what stands in our way. Eventually, we move past all of the *Stasis* points, to a place of consensus and common ground, and ultimately achieve an *Ideal Final Result.*

Things You Can Do

- Create a cheat sheet with definitions and bullets for both *Topoi* and *Stasis.*
- After the next disagreement you participate in, identify the *Stasis,* and see if identifying your sticking point or points might have helped you resolve the disagreement in a better way.
- Identify whether someone in a dispute is truly participating with you.
- The next time you have an argument, try to use one of the *Innovative Questions* in the fable and see if the outcome is different than you might have expected. ▪

CHAPTER 6

Is Change for You?

Men are anxious to improve their circumstances,
but are unwilling to improve themselves;
they therefore remain bound.

— JAMES ALLEN

After reading the "Storm" fable, you may find yourself having one of several different reactions. First, the easiest, "I'm going to try those ideas right away." Second, "I'm willing to try it, but I'm not sure if I can do it." And, third, "There's no way that's going to work for me."

Change is difficult. Certainly, if you are reading this book, change is in the air. You may want to change. You may have been told you need to change. You may think that everything is okay, yet something still tells you that all is not quite right with the way things are going. We believe that, since you are reading this book, you are looking to improve.

We classify change into three different categories:

1. Kaikaku
2. Kaizen
3. No Change

We have adopted these terms from a manufacturing process improvement program called Lean. Created in Japan, Lean seeks to make changes to improve organizational outcomes. According to Lean, there are two ways to go about making change: Kaikaku and Kaizen. Kaikaku is the process of making rapid, large-scale change in order to receive large gains. It's somewhat akin to bikini waxing — you rip off the wax quickly, and the change process is complete. Kaizen, on the other side, is the process of small changes which, in the end, add up to significant results.

Robert Maurer, in his book ***One Small Step Can Change Your Life: The Kaizen Way***[6], talks about the difference between innovation, what we call Kaikaku, and Kaizen. Maurer equates innovation to a breakthrough. He goes on to say that these changes almost never work. People fall back into their old habits. Instead, he recommends another path. Maurer quotes Lao Tzu:

A journey of a thousand miles must begin with the first step.

He goes on to say that the fear response, innately built into our human brains, gets in the way of large-scale change. Instead, he proposes:

Small, easily achievable goals — such as picking up and storing just one paperclip on a chronically messy desk — lets you tiptoe right past the amygdala [fear response], keeping it asleep and unable to set off alarm bells. As your steps continue and your cortex starts working, the brain begins to create "software" for

---

[6] Maurer, Robert. *One Small Step Can Change Your Life: The Kaizen Way*. Workman publishing. New York. 2004.

your desired change, actually laying down new nerve pathways in building new habits.

While we wish that the changes we propose were Kaizen for all of our readers, this is not the case in many situations. In fact, we find that not only do the suggestions sit along a continuum of easy to hard, the difficulty in implementing any one *Innovative Question* is also dependent on the individual.

For example, Chris was working with one of his clients, a CFO, and suggested that one of his goals should be to differentiate between opinion and fact and ask others to do the same. His client just loved the idea and started using it right away. It was easy for him to understand, it resonated with him, so it fell in the Kaizen category for him. This represented a small change, an option he just hadn't seen before, so there wasn't any struggle in getting started.

For individuals who find these changes to be Kaizen, *Innovative Questions* provide a way to make changes easily, a little bit at a time. And, you'll make these minor changes by simply selecting them from a menu. For example, instead of confronting a staff member by saying "I'm not happy with your performance," you will turn it around by asking a question like, "What did you learn from this experience, and how would you do it differently in the future?"

Others may not find a suggestion like this so easy. For example, if Chris were to suggest to a leader that they should try not to win every argument, he or she might answer, "I have to win every argument — that's how I make sure we are going in the right direction." For this leader, this would be a big change.

People find Kaikaku difficult because it represents a major change for them. Furthermore, what is Kaizen for one person is Kaikaku for another. One person may find it easy to get in front of an audience of 500; another may be terrified of any speech in public. The person who is terrified of public speaking may be perfectly fine giving a PowerPoint presentation to his team. We have found no formula for predicting what is Kaizen versus Kaikaku.

There are a number of reasons why a change can present itself as Kaikaku. First, the change can appear to be completely different than the manner in which the person is used to presenting him or herself. Second, the person can be afraid of how the change will manifest itself, either via the perception of others or the outcomes from the change. Finally, a person may out and out disagree with the change.

The Golf Story

So, what's the solution? How can you make significant change and make it stick? A simple story that helps illustrate this concept comes from Chris's desire to get better at golf. Chris was an okay golfer but was shooting in the mid-90s. He grew up as a caddie, so he understood the game and wanted to get better. Now, he's become good with "limited constraints." Several years ago, he was invited to play golf Wednesday mornings with some friends. He decided to take some lessons.

When he first started talking to the instructor, he was playing himself up. He told the instructor about his experience, what he thought he could do, how good he might get. The instructor had had enough of this, so he told him to take a few swings. After watching the swings, he said to Chris, "You've never had any lessons, have you?" When Chris replied that he hadn't, the instructor said, "It shows."

The instructor then said, "Can you explain the grip to me?" Chris didn't follow, so he said, somewhat flip, "you just grip it and rip it. The instructor asked, "Okay, tell me where the pressure points are." "I don't know," was Chris's response. The instructor then asked a question that's now part of Chris's repository: "How good do you want to be?" Chris's answer was, "I don't have a lot of time. I'm going to play about three times a month, and I'd like to be a single-digit handicap and be able to play to it."

The instructor's response was, "Great, that makes sense. Work on your grip first. Grip the club every day, 20 times a day, hands-on, hands-off, and think about the pressure points. Keep the pressure off the pinky finger of your right hand. If we have to, we'll use a popsicle stick and tape to keep it off."

When Chris came back for his next lesson and then started swinging, the instructor asked, "Did you practice your grip?" Chris came up with several excuses. The instructor retorted with a similar answer to before, "It shows…. Look, I'm perfectly happy to keep taking your money, but if you truly want to get better, you're going to need to practice what you learn from me."

Now, Chris takes a club with him, even to this day, every time he goes out with his dog, every time he walks with his wife. The result: He's a nine handicap. Translation: He's a pretty good golfer. The upshot: significant change requires practice, motivation and discipline. Chris likes to quote Aristotle in these types of situations: "We are what we repeatedly do. Excellence is not an act, but a habit."

For those individuals who find *Innovative Questions* to be Kaikaku, major change, we fully understand. Even if a leader finds asking a new question easy, other aspects of the process may not be. Change and sustaining change is not an easy process for almost anyone, because discomfort usually accompanies change, even if it's for the better.

Effecting change also requires accepting stepping out of your comfort zone. Often in the coaching process, people say to Chris, "I don't want to do that." Or, they say, "That would make me uncomfortable." Chris's answer: "If you are looking for a coach who is going to make you feel comfortable, I am not your guy." In fact, one client who turned down his services told the human resources person that the openness of communicating what you are working on to improve, including stakeholders and measuring effectiveness, all parts of Chris' process, scared him.

Undoubtedly, leaders must be motivated to change in some way and be able to see and articulate the benefits of the change. Companies undertake Kaikaku, large-scale change, for a number of reasons. In most cases, something is truly broken. In other cases, large rewards can be reaped. We can apply the same concepts to motivating individuals to make this type of change, scary, uncomfortable, or not.

How to Make the Change

So how do you get started with change? First, we suggest picking an easy task for you on the continuum of change. Remember, using *Innovative Questions* does require foundational elements. So, as you are choosing which ones of these to start with, think carefully. If one task is too large for you, pick something that's easier. Instead of taking on "not having to win every argument," perhaps you can try "looking for what you agree with" or "not interrupting." Alternatively, you might try not having the last word in a conversation. These might be much more akin for you to picking up a paperclip than other changes. Find the smallest change, and begin with that.

Chris provides a number of different strategies for those individuals who are not immediately willing to try something or find it difficult to make changes. Consider the following scenarios:

Client says: I'm not capable of changing.

Chris says: I'm sure you could make that a self-fulfilling prophecy.

Client says: I'm not sure I can do this.

Chris asks: Do you think you have the potential to do this?

Client says: That will never work in this company.
Chris asks: If you had a magic wand and could change one thing to make it work, what would it be?

Each of these methods works to turn around the client's blockade and creates the space to think differently. As an aside, if one of these phrases resonates with you, or you think it will help with those individuals with whom you interact, keep it in the back of your head, and try it to see if it works. As a suggestion, David likes to write down new questions to ask on his task list so he remembers to use them when the opportunity arises.

Using Perspective

Once a client comes on board and presents themselves as open to learning and trying new things, Chris uses different perspectives to begin the change process. Acting provides one medium for getting to this point. By using your imagination, you can learn how to properly implement IQs. Here's an example:

> You are speaking to someone who has a Doberman Pinscher right at their side. If you raised your voice, the dog would attack you. So, you must speak calmly and softly and keep that dog from attacking you.

Also, leaders can think about their situation from a movie perspective: What does the protagonist want? What's keeping him from getting it? What does he have to do to get it? Chris then frames the improvement process in terms that make his client the protagonist. For example, his client wants to move up in the company. He's not moving up in the company because of his behavior. One of the ways he can achieve this is to listen to other people's opinions without interrupting. Keeping this in mind, he can focus on the need to change.

Involving Others

When David was learning to systematically remove the word "but" from his vocabulary, Chris suggested that he involve others in his change process. At the beginning of a meeting, he said, "Why don't you tell people what you are trying to do, and they can call you on it when you say the word 'but.'" When Chris teaches classes, he will often put down a dollar bill that will go to a local charity every time he says "but" and on a subsequent day, ask his students to participate in the same way.

An apology can also be highly effective while working on the change process. For example, if someone's trying not to interrupt, and he finds that he does, the leader can say, "I apologize. I'm trying to work on this, and I would appreciate if you would bring it to my attention if you find I'm interrupting." While this does take courage, discipline, and humility, it's highly effective in getting you to change.

Making a Habit

Chris provides his clients another tool, the daily sheet. Each day, the client uses the daily sheet to capture what they did that day on their improvement items. The daily sheet keeps the idea in the prefrontal cortex part of our brain — the part of our brain that we use to remember things we are learning. By familiarizing the mind with the task, the daily sheet helps get past the brain's fear response and enables the skill to become a new habit.

Another good way to get people to help you change is to rehearse what you are going to say to them. Chris was working with a senior leader to rehearse what he was going to say to a group of peers. In front of the senior leadership, including the division president, he said:

As many of you know, I have been the recipient of a 360°
evaluation. Your feedback, as well as that of others, was that
I needed to listen more, collaborate better, incorporate other
people's ideas into the final decision, and that I need to treat
people better. In the past, I know that I have not done these
things as well as I should have and that I have not always
treated people with respect. If you been the recipient of such
behavior, I apologize, and I commit to do better with your help.

What did this accomplish? First, it let people know that he was
willing to change. His words and feelings were earnest, and he had
his audience's full, focused attention. You could hear a pin drop in
the room when he spoke. Second, it took a lot of courage. In fact, a
number of people made comments at the retreat about how much
courage it took to stand in front of that group and make that kind of
statement. Third, other people would now be more likely to remind
the leader of when he was going outside of his commitment. Finally,
by apologizing sincerely, he conveyed how badly he felt about what
had happened in the past and that he truly wanted to make a change
for the better.

The comment from the leader himself: "It was the hardest thing
I've ever done. I agonized about it for two days." It was simple to
understand but most certainly not easy to actually do. We want to
remind our readers that while the concepts in this book may be simple,
some of them may be difficult to enact. As we hope we will show you,
the results are well worth the work.

Simple or complex, easy or hard, if you are reading this book, we
know that you want to change something about the way you interact
with others and how those subsequent outcomes unfold. If you find,
as you are reading these pages, that some of these ideas are difficult to
implement, we suggest that you come back to this chapter and use one

of the techniques outlined here to help you begin your implementation of that suggestion.

Things You Can Do

- Ask yourself why you are doing something. What's your intention in doing this? If you find yourself answering that your intention is to win or another negative behavior, think about trying something else.
- Watch the reaction of the other people in the room. If you find them looking concerned about something you just said, ask them about it. You might get a clue as to their perceived reaction of your intention.

CHAPTER 7

Getting It

n this book, there are two levels of *Getting It* — meaning truly understanding, embracing, and being able to execute *Innovative Questions*.
First, the leader needs to embrace the idea that changing her engagement with others and sustaining that change benefits herself (the
leader). Second, the recipients of the leader's behavior need to see that
change, see that the individual is working toward competence in the
change, acknowledge it and, perhaps most importantly, understand
that it will be helpful to them personally as well.

How do we achieve these outcomes? By doing it repeatedly and
subsequently seeing the benefit. Confucius says:

> I hear and I forget.
> I see and I remember.
> I **do** and I **understand**

In other words, in order for someone to truly absorb the benefits
of a change, we have to move the change from the prefrontal lobe of
the brain to the basal ganglia or the hard wiring of the brain. In order
to make this happen, we need to make the benefit apparent to the
person who is trying to change. For a leader to sustain change, the end
result must be important to them, and they must be able to articulate

the benefit of the eventual outcome. Understanding the reward more quickly inserts the skill into our hard wiring — it becomes part of our behavioral DNA.

The next step centers on practice. The leader must practice the skill to truly become competent. To this end, Chris has his clients fill out a "daily sheet," as we mentioned in the last chapter and which we have included at the end of the book in Appendix B. On this sheet, each client simply indicates which of their goals they worked on for that particular day. For the reader of this book, that can be as simple as asking whether or not you used an *Innovative Question* today in dealing with others.

Story: Quitting Smoking

Here's a story that helps us illustrate the difficulty of sustaining change. Chris's brother-in-law said he was going to quit smoking after Chris's younger sister died of cancer at age 52. Curt said quitting is easy. "I've quit 30 to 40 times," he said. It's sustaining it that's difficult.

We believe that change boils down to a cost/benefit analysis: "When I get better at 'listening to different points of view with an open mind before giving my opinion,' the benefits to me will be…."

Steps of Getting It

In figuring out these benefits, here's a series of steps we believe people follow when they learn and retain skills and habits:

1. Find the motivation to try something new.
2. Understand the costs and benefits of achieving the goal.
3. Learn what to do.
4. Develop the skills to do it.
5. Acknowledge that you have changed and realize the benefit.

Let's walk through how these steps actually work. First, you have to have the motivation to try something new. Otherwise, there would be no attempt to learn it at all. If everything is going fine, why change? However, if you are being told you could benefit from working with a coach, maybe now you have some motivation — perhaps your career momentum is in jeopardy. If you are having some seriously confrontational meetings, then perhaps you are motivated to try a new way. If your personal relationships are suffering, if you just want to be the best leader you can be, you definitely have some motivation.

Second, you need to understand the costs and benefits of making any change. If it's easy to do and has a large gain, why not? On the other hand, something exceptionally hard to do that doesn't result in much positive outcome — well maybe you want to reconsider attempting that change.

You will then need to learn what to do and how to do it. Conceptually, you may understand what you need to do, but you have to know how to execute. Ultimately, you will need to acquire the skills to do it well. Of course, there is the bonus of recognizing the achievement and realizing the benefit of a positive change.

Let's apply this sequence of *Getting It* to *Innovative Questions*. If you are reading this book, you probably have some motivation to try something new. Otherwise, you could be doing something more productive or fun, like getting a massage or playing golf. If you've gotten this far in the book, you at least suspect that there is some benefit to what we are proposing. So now, you have to try a question, get better at asking it in the right situation, and eventually become practiced at using a particular question.

Here's an example with one of our favorite questions. "Is it possible that the opposite of what you said is true?" It's easy to ask the question. Learning what to do is easy. Knowing the right way to apply the question is, on the other hand, the topic of this book.

Story: The Business Tiger

We can illustrate this point through a story. One of Chris's clients, Stephen, was known as a tiger in business. When he got his first set of feedback, he got very low scores. He said to Chris, "I'm not like this at home." Chris suggested that they call his wife and ask her what she thought. Her answer was what you might expect: "That's absolutely how you are here." Stephen still disagreed. Chris then said, "Would you like to call one of your teenage kids?" Stephen answered, "No."

Stephen still hadn't decided whether or not to retain Chris as his coach, but his wife decided to help the situation. She said, "I'd like you to observe our older son's basketball game." When the game was over, she asked, "What were your observations?" Stephen said that he was kind of a bully. And, she responded, "Where do you think he learned that behavior?"

The next day, Chris received a phone call from Stephen asking him to engage as his coach. When Chris asked what helped Stephen make up his mind, he said, "If someone like you were giving my son a feedback report like mine in 20 years, I'd be ashamed of the job I've done as a father. I'd like your help." Stephen found the motivation to change.

Methods of Motivation

Different people gain motivation in different ways. Someone who has perfectionist tendencies might be more willing to try something because of the potential benefit, whereas someone else might stay in their comfort zone. Additionally, if someone feels uncomfortable with doing something and they have a choice, they typically won't do anything. They'd prefer to stay right where they are.

Here's a quotation from James Allen that we find particularly apropos:

Humans are anxious to improve their circumstances, but generally unwilling to improve themselves; therefore we remain where we are.

In Marshall Goldsmith's book, *Mojo*, he states:

Our default reaction in life is to not experience happiness, is not to experience meaning, but to experience inertia.[7]

How do we turn someone from inertia to motivation? We help people change by helping them see the benefit to them. We can help them see the benefit to them by giving them the opportunity to see something from a different perspective. *Innovative Questions* works on both of these levels: By allowing another perspective and by providing an enormous benefit in the outcome.

Remember, in the process of *Getting It*, once you've achieved motivation, you next assess the costs and benefits of the desired change. In our scenario, we would like to think that the cost is pretty small. You might feel silly making a particular statement, or you might be worried that someone will get upset because you are rocking their applecart. Chris has repeatedly shown that, with *Innovative Questions*, the downside is very small. In fact, we have found quite the opposite to be true. *Innovative Questions* have a very large upside.

Think about this. We have repeatedly and consistently found the benefits of using *Innovative Questions* to be very significant. Maybe you have a meeting that doesn't turn confrontational. Maybe people walk out of a meeting feeling good instead of bad. Maybe you get to

---

[7] Goldsmith, Marshall. *Mojo: How to Get It, How to Keep It, How to Get It Back if You Lose It!*. Hyperion, 2010.

go home feeling happy instead of frustrated. All of a sudden, one after the other, Chris's clients have seen the benefits and want to try more.

In the next step, once you've decided to take the action, you need to have the skills to do it. And that is the ultimate goal of this book. We will teach you how to apply the questions for maximum benefit.

Finally, once you have mastered each skill, you can then see the benefit in action. You implemented a question, and it has worked for you. As you see the benefits pouring in, you will try more and more *Innovative Questions*. Your life will get better, and your outcomes will improve.

Getting it is the primary key in learning. Once someone gets a taste of a benefit of a particular change, they want to go back for more. It feels good to improve, and it feels better to be happy. Let's take some more steps down the road of *Innovative Questions.*

Human Nature

Change the Behavior

To function in society effectively, we must be able to control our behavior. To those who think that they are unable to change their behavior, we beg to differ: Humans can learn to think and process information differently and affect their resultant behavior. Chris's methods systematically allow individuals the *Safe Space* to change their reactions to stimuli and get better at specifically identified behaviors. Not only can we change our behaviors, research has shown that changing our behaviors also changes the way we think and feel.[8] As author Richard Pascale puts it:

> People are much more likely to act their way into a new way of thinking, than think their way into a new way of acting.[9]

Here's how it works — because behavior is a response to an activating event, humans can be trained to change their reaction to that event. Because behavior is observable, one person can give feedback to another as to what their future voluntary behavior might be.

---

[8] For example, *http://en.wikipedia.org/wiki/Positive_Deviance, http://radar.oreilly.com/ 2006/09/act-your-way-into-a-new-way-of.html.*
[9] Pascale, Richard, *Delivering Results,* Harvard business review, Boston, 1998.

Innovative Questions provides a mechanism for allowing leaders to change the way they behave and think and in turn create an environment in which the behaviors of those around them can change for the better.

Are you the smartest person in the room?

Most of Chris's clients are extremely bright and highly educated. In many cases, they are said to be the smartest person in the room. If the only thing that outcomes depended upon was a single smart leader making all of the decisions, you would not be reading this book. By the time most of his clients get to Chris, the establishment of whether or not they are smart and successful already happened quite a long time ago. The *Stasis* point of the problem now usually centers on interaction with others. In fact, most of the time, team frustrations center on the lack of satisfying interactions with the individual leader.

Since you are reading this book, we are certain that you can envision how many of your conversations with others could be more productive and positive. To be honest, we are not concerned about who is responsible for a less-than-optimal outcome. We are not attributing blame to anyone, and we are not interested in who is to blame. We are proposing, though, that you have the capability to rise above these problems by changing your engagement with them.

Do not be fooled into believing that you cannot make a difference on your own. One who is skilled in the art of conversation can truly improve the result of almost any interaction.

Human Conflict Management

Since this chapter talks about human nature, the authors wanted to bring in one of their favorite sources on conflict management in supporting the benefit of the *Innovative Question* methodology. Since

Innovative Questions center around making conflict constructive, we thought it would be beneficial to insert some summary material from a course we both enjoyed.

Four Goals Revisited

In his course entitled "The Art of Conflict Management," offered through the Great Courses, Michael Dues talks about four different goals of conflict. We will be referring to information in this series of lectures throughout the chapter.[10]

We first presented these goals in the Storm fable, and we want to cover them in a little bit more depth here. These four goals are simultaneously operating in any discussion or conflict:

1. Topic goal: What's the actual point of discussion? What do the words say you are trying to achieve?
2. Relationship goal: What's the relationship that the parties in the discussion want to have between each other?
3. Identity goal: How are the parties' identities maintained through the discussion? How does an individual want to be seen, and how are they seen?
4. Process goal: What's the process for the discussion look like?

Either consciously or unconsciously, these four goals exist in every conflict. Being aware of their existence helps you understand why *Innovative Questions* function so effectively. Here's where a real-life case study would be helpful in demonstrating how these goals operate.

---

[10] Dues, Michael. *The Art of Conflict Management: Achieving Solutions for Life, Work, and Beyond.* Chantilly, VA: The Teaching Company, 2010. Available at *www.thegreat courses.com.*

Four Goals Case Study

While working out this chapter, David had a situation with one of his team leaders that helped clarify the importance of understanding human nature. David was working with Neil, one of his staff members, on a project to change the way the membership department was going to bill dues to its members. The business unit found that a number of customers were frustrated that they didn't understand how their membership dues worked when they were also being billed for other fees at other times. As a result, the organization decided that it was going to bill all of these charges at the same time.

David understood that the business unit needed to make this change. Neil felt that he should have been consulted before the change was made. They ended up in a situation where Neil said that it was not possible to implement even an intermediate solution within the six weeks until the system went live.

David mapped out the four goals with Neil. It went something like this:

Topic: Did we meet the needs of the clients?

Relationship: Was Neil respected by the business unit and David by not being consulted before the decision was made?

Identity: Neil wanted to be thought of as someone who is effective in meeting his goals and creating good, quality solutions. Neil wanted to feel that he was an important part of the process.

Process: How was the decision made? Was it prudent to continue to support older software? Was everyone who should be included consulted before the decision was made?

By delving beyond just the seemingly simple topical goal, David was able to unearth some useful and fairly strong feelings. Neil was feeling frustrated and angry with the way he felt he was being treated. Other items that came out of this discussion with Neil included a frustration with apparently changing ground rules, a flip-flop on the part of IT policy, and not liking the feeling of being surprised. By bringing this to the surface, these issues could be addressed. These feelings can also get in the way of effective behaviors, such as being angry about one thing and displaying it in another area. David was also able to see that he could have significantly improved in his handling of the situation.

Understanding that there is more to a decision-making process than the end result in any given interaction helps leaders make those interactions more satisfying for those involved and achieve more desirable outcomes. *Innovative Questions* support these four goals of conflict by addressing the needs of our collaboration partners.

Clarity and Contribution

Since a basic tenet of *Innovative Questions* is *Clarity Is Power*, the more clarity we have on the situation, the better. In essence, we must remember that there are many things going on at the same time as we process through conflict, and one of the things of which we should be aware are the feelings and goals of everyone involved. Many *Innovative Questions* allow for feelings to be brought to the surface, thereby allowing us to understand what needs to be addressed in each instance.

Innovative Questions also give us the ability to better provide a framework in which people can contribute to the total picture. A coach works to influence leaders' behaviors in a positive direction. In turn, leaders can create a space for more effective behaviors. This works on two levels: First, *Safe Space* opens up the door for people to participate. Secondly, when people participate and feel valued, they are more likely to contribute to an effective outcome.

Perspective

Building on our understanding of human nature, we would like to present several tenets of conflict management which are critical to the successful use of *Innovative Questions*. First, human beings understand the world from a particular perspective. That means that reality doesn't always coincide with the perspective that you believe is accurate.

For example, if you haven't always protected your staff as they would have liked, your motivations are going to come across as suspect, even if your words say you have their best interests in mind. If you've always interrupted people at meetings and not listened to their opinions, they're going to have a specific perception when they enter a meeting with you. Even if you listen without interrupting and tell people you understand their point of view, if you still never defer to someone else's opinion, they will see you are not open to changing your mind based upon what they say. And, for the many reasons we have already discussed, that is just going to make them feel upset and angry.

Two skills that we believe are important when interacting with others are empathy (the skill to be able to understand what another person is experiencing) and perspective-taking (adapting a viewpoint that considers how events might look and feel to another person). We would like you to think about the possibility that someone else has a different perspective than you and that it's helpful to try to see things through their eyes. Similarly, trying to be empathetic can help you see the other person's point of view and how they came to their decision or position.

We have a couple of questions that might help you with these situations. In the case where you see that someone else has a different perspective from you, try saying, "Help me understand your point of view," or "How did you get to your position?" As we discussed in the fable, for empathy, you can look for things that you agree with when having a conversation with another person. You can also rephrase back what you are hearing about how that person feels. Additionally, you can articulate what you agree with, point out where you see things differently, ask the person what you have missed, and then give them an opportunity to further elaborate and clarify their point of view. To put it another way, try to allow yourself to be convinced of the other person's point of view. And, most importantly, if it is indeed valid, do whatever you can to incorporate it in the final decision.

Emotions

As we have already discussed, emotions form a significant part of how human beings interact. For example, while human beings often perceive themselves as being rational beings with emotions, current research shows that the opposite is most likely true. Human beings are most likely emotional beings who have evolved the ability to occasionally reason.[11]

While delving into the emotional state of human beings is far beyond the scope of what we hope to accomplish here, we want you to remember that emotions are part of human existence and that they occur in reaction to something else. Dues points out that there are two central elements of emotions:

- The feeling itself.
- The intensity of the feeling or arousal.

---

[11] See for example, Brafman, Ori and Brafman, Rom, *Sway: The Irresistible Pull of Irrational Behavior*, Random House Digital, Inc., 2008

This means that, for any particular emotion, humans have an associated feeling and, that feeling can range from mild to very strong. Emotions are part of being a human being, and they don't require apologies. As leaders, we must understand that people are entitled to their emotions, and supporting them while emotional goes a long way toward building relationships.

Given the importance of supporting individuals during an emotional time, here are some strategies for dealing with emotions during conflict:

- Report them to the other party. "I can see that you are very upset right now."
- Understand that an emotion is not a "judgment about the other party or you."
- Use "I" statements.
- Use a timeout technique to take a pause if the arousal level is too high.

Emotional Rights

Additionally, you and your teams need to know that you all have a right to the following:

- Feeling emotions.
- An environment in which it is safe to talk about emotions. Remember, you are trying to create a *Safe Space* in which decisions can be made.
- Someone "who is willing to listen, work out the conflict and create an acceptable solution for both sides."

These three elements are very important to *Innovative Questions*. First, emotions are part of day-to-day human experience, and if we want to create a *Safe Space,* we should never say things like, "You don't have the right to feel that emotion." Second, leaders benefit when we allow our team members and stakeholders a *Safe Space* to talk about their emotions. Condemning or dismissing those emotions only makes a conflict worse. We strongly believe that someone should be allowed to express their feelings and the impact they are having on them. We also don't believe that they should be allowed to ramble on for 20 or 30 minutes. If you do find that a discussion about emotions is going on too long, make sure you ask your conversational partner questions like, "What should we do next?" or "How were you hoping I could help you here?" In summary, providing a *Safe Space* to discuss emotions makes managers even more effective and is an essential part of IQs.

Third, leaders have an obligation to work through a conflict. By working through a conflict, we get better clarity, and we get a better outcome. As we saw from our fable, the outcome that comes from working within a *Safe Space* gets us to our most ideal result. Also, because conflict in a *Safe Space* is by definition collaborative, people walk out of that conflict feeling better, even if their topical goal has not been met. When discussing this outcome with his clients, Chris often tells his leaders often that they should disagree without being disagreeable.

Chris often works with his clients on the concept of being a willing partner in conversations, dialogue, and execution of tasks. Throughout his engagements, Chris reminds his clients that being a willing partner requires courage, caring, and humility. Showing a willingness to be a true partner is just one more way that you create *Safe Sp*ace for your team members.

As a leader, we urge you to think about how you will be perceived if you cannot achieve a partner/leader role. If you cannot find the courage to address difficult feelings and take steps to repair them, you will most likely find your relationships strained with your subordinates. If you can't understand that there is another person on the other side of the conflict, with their own needs and aspirations, you will have more and bigger bumps in the way of achieving your outcomes. Instead, we propose that you try the opposite of this: Constantly remind yourself that there is another person on the other side of the conflict and that the two of you can strive together toward an outcome that works for both of you.

Chris often reminds his clients to fly in the face of conventional wisdom. It does not take two to have an effective conversation; it takes one who is skilled enough to guide the dialogue and the debate so that a win-win resolution can be achieved. You can be that skilled individual.

Power

Individuals are susceptible to power differentials. As a leader, we want you to think about the leverage that you have over other individuals, as well as how others have leverage over you, and how misusing that power can lead to significant consequences. As a leader, you always have the opportunity to use your position power to make a decision. In fact, that's one of the reasons why Chris is often called in to coach an individual. Power can strip subordinates of winning on topic, process, identity, or relationship goals. We urge that you take just the opposite position and give up some of your position power for a more positive outcome.

Interdependence

Additionally, individuals who have a conflict are, by definition, interdependent. If two individuals are not reliant on each other, there is no need for conflict. Just because two people think different things doesn't mean anything needs to come of it. For example, if someone on the street says to you that they don't agree with your political point of view, you can simply say, "Thank you for sharing your point of view" and move on.

In the employer/employee relationship, your staff is reliant upon you in many ways. First, they rely upon you to continue to allow them to work. Second, they are looking for appreciation and good feedback. And, third, they want to be part of the decision-making equation. As part of their identity, they want to count. The bottom line: Everyone wants to feel significant, confident, and likable.

On the other hand, you rely on your team members to execute on your vision. If you recall, Cicero's vision for a leader included the ability to get others to execute on the leader's vision. If your staff members don't execute, you don't look good, either.

Because you and your staff are interdependent on each other, leaders must understand the power differential that they hold and use it wisely. This also makes it important to understand the perspective from which you are coming and from which you are perceived. As a leader, how people perceive you directly correlates with your ability to be effective.

Win-Win

In his lectures, Dues introduces the Thomas-Kilmann Conflict Style Model. This model details five different styles ranging across two continuums from passive to assertive and uncooperative to cooperative:[12]

---

[12] Dues, Michael. *The Art of Conflict Management: Achieving Solutions for Life, Work, and Beyond.* Chantilly, VA: The Teaching Company, 2010.

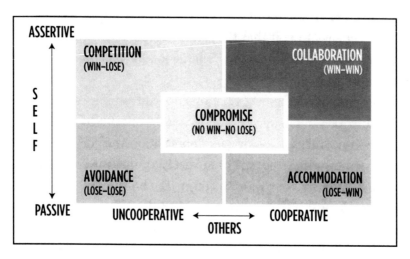

Figure 8.1 Thomas-Kilmann conflict style model

The Conflict Style Model helps leaders understand the benefit of acting in both assertive and cooperative ways when looking to resolve conflict. Let's take a look at the various scenarios in the model and how understanding them can help a leader create win-win outcomes. Let's start with avoidance. Avoiding the situation simply leads to lose-lose. No one can win here. Have you ever tried to completely ignore a problem with the hope that it will go away? How did that work out for you?

With competition, someone needs to win, as is the case with its evil twin, accommodation, where someone needs to lose. With compromise, nobody gets what they want in the end, so it clearly is not the most effective path. With all of those out of the way, the Conflict Style model hypothesizes that, with collaboration, everyone's goals or intentions can be accounted for, and a true win-win can be strived for and developed.

How is this achieved? When developing win-win outcomes, individuals in the conflict don't look only at the desired outcome; they need to look at the underlying goals of each individual involved.

When everyone asserts their own needs and cooperates with each other, a true collaboration can come together.

Roger Fisher and William Ury from the Harvard Negotiation Project did a lot of work on learning how to create win-win outcomes. Ury and Fisher have developed five principles for win-win negotiations:[13]

1. Focus on behaviors or events rather than the parties involved.
2. Focus on interests, not positions.
3. Generate options for mutual gain.
4. Base the choice on some sort of objective criteria.
5. Understand what to do if the negotiation fails.

The first of these principles talks about making sure you are speaking about behaviors and not the individual. For example, telling someone that they are a terrible employee is not helpful. On the other hand, telling them that they have to improve their work or behavior in a specific area with examples can be quite beneficial.

Second, remember that people have both interests and positions. An interest is a goal a person is trying to achieve. On the other hand, a position is what the person is saying they want in the end out of that particular discussion. It's important, as we have already discussed, to achieve clarity on the *Ideal Final Result*, and the same applies here. Clarity needs to be achieved not only on the intended result but also on the result for the individuals involved.

After understanding interests (or goals), individuals can work on multiple options that can bring wins for both parties. After multiple options are determined, a decision can be made, ideally based upon objective criteria determined before the decision is made.

---

[13] *http://en.wikipedia.org/wiki/Getting_to_YES.*

Finally, individuals need to understand (in the Ury and Fisher model) what they're going to do if the negotiation fails. We hope this doesn't occur with *Innovative Questions,* however, the possibility of a failed negotiation exists, and you should think about what you are going to do if that happens.

Behavior and Negotiation

There are two other elements required in order to resolve a conflict. Both are critical to *Innovative Questions*:

1. An issue must be defined in terms of "voluntary behavior from the present moment forward."
2. The other party "must be willing and able to negotiate" to an outcome.[14]

Both of these are cornerstone features of *Innovative Questions.* As a coach, Chris helps people change the way they behave. Why? Because conflict resolution works by identifying how we decide on a voluntary behavior moving forward. When people are asking for a change from you, they are asking for a behavior, one different than the type of behavior you have exhibited previously.

Secondly, Chris does not take on clients who are not willing to change or don't see any need to improve. In this context, we refer to the fact that leaders who need to get better need to negotiate what they're going to work on and how they're going to get better. If they are not willing, the outcome will not be positive. And, certainly, if they are

---

[14] Dues, Michael. *The Art of Conflict Management: Achieving Solutions for Life, Work, and Beyond.* Chantilly, VA: The Teaching Company, 2010, p. 45.

not able to agree to a change, meaning they cannot control themselves, they are not going to get anywhere near a positive outcome. We could, of course, debate all day long whether "not able" means "not willing," but that stands well beyond the scope of this book.

The same applies to leaders managing their subordinates. Since emotions can't be easily regulated, and thinking can't be seen, behaviors are the best way to see and evaluate a definitive outcome. While emotions or thoughts are certainly part of the equation, they are impossible to quantitatively measure. That doesn't mean you and others won't end up feeling better in the end. In Chris's model, thinking and feeling can actually follow behavioral changes once they are firmly entrenched in a person's operating modality. A number of management theorists also argue a strong case that you can act your way into a new way of thinking.

In summary, now that we understand that sustained behavioral change that is recognized and acknowledged by others is the goal of a negotiation, we want to add two more points. First, building upon what we discussed earlier in this chapter, individuals must understand their goals and seek to understand the goals of the person with whom they are negotiating. Second, while the goal of a negotiation is to achieve win-win, sometimes a reasonable result cannot be achieved via negotiation. In the end, if you don't think that you can negotiate, or the negotiation does not end in the way you want, you need to consider what your best alternative might be, also known as BATANA (Best Alternative to a Negotiated Agreement).

Conflict, Win-Win, and Negotiation

We summarize how conflict, win-win, and negotiation all work together in the following diagram:

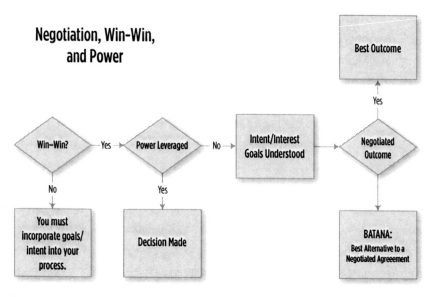

Figure 8.2

Each conflict first starts out with whether or not the parties are willing to engage from a win-win perspective. If not, a ground rule must be established that the goals and intents of all parties must be considered.

Second, from our perspective, it's critical that you avoid using the power of your position to make a decision. Use your position power as judiciously and as infrequently as necessary. Otherwise, the decision is just "made," and people are left flat from the perspective of a number of their goals. As we've mentioned, a large number of people have been handed a coach specifically for not including others in the decision-making process, either overtly or more covertly by simply ignoring an individual's contributions. Remember, this may not be about the reality of the situation; the perceptions of others are critical.

Third, once we've gotten through these two requirements of win-win and not unduly using power, we are well on our way to understanding the intent and interest goals, and we are able to negotiate well. If negotiation goes well, the best outcome can be reached; otherwise, we need to consider what the best alternative might be. In the end, if we use this path to reinforce *Innovative Questions,* we are well on the way to improved outcomes.

Differences of Perception

Understanding human nature also demands that we be cognizant of differences in perception. Dues talks about the difference of perception using the example of communicating the word "tree" to show us that the perception of what a listener receives is always different than what a speaker sends. For example, if I say the word "tree" to someone with whom I'm having a conversation, they may picture a pine tree when I'm talking about an oak tree. Dues suggests using listening skills to better be able to decipher the messages that are being sent to you and to help the other party decipher the message you are sending to them. Using listening skills allows you to best select an appropriate *Innovative Question* in a particular situation.

There are a number of ways to make sure you are fully focusing on the task of listening. True focusing can be quite difficult, so it's helpful to set a time limit for the communication, pay undivided attention, and capture what is said. It's also quite important to paraphrase the message back, which we call "clarifying and confirming." This cannot be by simply parroting the message. It is essential that you restate the message in your own words and concepts.

We also want to impress upon you the importance of helping the listener process and understand the message you are trying to convey. Not everyone with whom you work will be effective at conveying their message or understanding what they want to get to. *Innovative Questions* give you the tools to help them get what they want as well. Remember, your ability to facilitate a conversation helps both you and the participants achieve their goals.

Rule of Reciprocity

Another useful human nature tool is the rule of reciprocity. By nature, humans want to be equal participants and be treated fairly. As we are processing through various *Innovative Questions*, you will notice that leaders and their partners are equal participants in the conversation. We want to impress that this is an important part of practicing the questions.

Difficult Messages

If you are trying to convey a difficult message, putting the listener at ease and softening the blow of the message as much as possible helps create *Safe Space* and allow for the message to be received openly. Allowing for breaks during difficult conversations also maintains *Safe Space*.

If you've done your job well, people will realize you are earnest and trying to help. Then, when you get to the time for difficult messages, they can be effectively processed by your stakeholders. You've created the foundation and the environment so they can receive these messages well and for them to improve.

Appreciation

As part of their identity goal, human beings have a definitive need for appreciation. As part of your job description as a manager and a leader, we urge you to say, "Thank you" quickly and often and be genuine in your appreciation. If you are not recognizing your staff for their good work, you are not going to be fulfilling one of their goals and needs.[15]

As you engage with your stakeholders, they need to believe that they are appreciated. Cicero also wrote, "Gratitude is not only the greatest of virtues, but the parent of all the others." When individuals feel that you are grateful for what they have done, they want to do more for you and with you. They also feel appreciated.

Happiness

Chris likes to sign his e-mails with the following quotation:

Be Happy Now

Another reminder of happiness as part of *Safe Space* comes from Eleanor Roosevelt:

Happiness is not a goal; it is a by-product.

This concept works on multiple levels. First, for your teams, they will be happier and more likely to do your work when you are grateful for theirs. Second, you will be happier when you open up to the feeling of gratitude when you understand how hard your team works for you.

Involvement

People naturally want to be involved. When you make decisions without including them, they can become frustrated. First, your decisions will most likely involve them. Second, you are affecting their relationship and identity goals with the manner in which you make

---

[15] Adapted from *Encouraging Development Steps*, copyright 2003 Frank Wagner, Chris Coffey and Marshall Goldsmith.

decisions. Involving them makes them feel valued. And, third, people want to be heard, understood, and have their ideas fairly considered.

We have a few thoughts about involving your stakeholders:

- Get them involved in negotiation of their roles. People like to be involved in their destiny.
- All stakeholders, regardless of position, have power bases they can develop and use to influence up, down, and across organizations. Even the lowest-ranking individual in your organization can help change the perception of others and be helpful to your cause.
- Asking others for their opinion and actually considering them is complimentary to them and helps gain a better outcome.
- Remember to engage with stakeholders using Cicero's philosophy. When people see you acting without a moral compass, for example, without integrity, they will assume you might behave poorly with regard to them as well.

Lastly, Chris repeatedly teaches his clients to learn to defer to other points of view. Deferring to others provides an exceptional method of inclusion. First, others will be grateful for the opportunity to participate with their idea. Second, you will give others the opportunity to grow, learn, and become more independent and confident in their ability to execute. Third, they will tend to work harder to execute their idea than yours.

Summary

Innovative Questions support the human elements of all the people with whom you interact. We want them to succeed, feel good, and participate. When their human needs are met:

- They are more capable of having their goals and intents met.
- They have a more positive perception of you as a leader and manager and more closely feel the bonds of a mutual relationship.
- They can be more effective in implementing your vision.

Human beings are complex and tend to be more emotional than rational. As a result, they look to their leader to help fulfill their human needs in their day-to-day work life. By being cognizant of their human nature, you can be more effective as their leader and mentor and help guide them to the best decision.

Things You Can Do
- Be cognizant of human nature when practicing *Innovative Questions.*
- Paraphrase what you are hearing back to your conversational partner.
- Ask your team members if they felt safe to share their feelings during the preceding meeting.

CHAPTER 9

Pulling Toward You or Pushing Away

"Tact is the ability to describe others as they see themselves."

— ABRAHAM LINCOLN

In the last chapter, we touched on human nature as a critical element in human interactions. In this chapter, we will focus on one specific element of how we interrelate with each other. In each interaction with another, you can either pull someone toward you or push them away. Pulling someone toward you means you are creating a *Safe Space* for them to interact with you. By pulling someone toward you, you help them feel that you have their best interests at heart, you are coming from a place of integrity, and you are willing to listen to them. On the other hand, pushing someone away makes them feel unsafe, undervalued, and unwilling to work with you.

Here's the example that Chris used when first explaining this concept. David has a conversation with one of his team members, Susan. Susan is sitting in a guest chair; David is sitting behind his desk. David's arms are crossed, and he is leaning back in his chair. He is frowning. David is pushing Susan away.

Alternatively, David pulls up a chair next to Susan. He leans slightly forward, listening attentively. He nods as she speaks and feeds back what she says accurately. David is pulling Susan toward him.

In any given conversation, we want you to continually consider whether you pull someone toward you or push them away. People don't like to be pushed away. It doesn't feel good to them. Pushing someone away can also be turning them against you. Making people your allies is far more productive than creating situations where individuals work against you. We separated this chapter from the previous one because of the importance of pulling someone toward you and how *Innovative Questions* help you achieve this goal.

Four Messages of Communication

A critical aspect of conflict management that we saved for this chapter centers around the four messages received in communication. I.A. Richards cites four elements which are at work in human communications:[16]

1. Sense: the actual words that are spoken.
2. Feeling: e.g., anger or disinterest; an underlying part of the message.
3. Tone: centers on the relationship between the speakers, for example, if one is talking down to another.
4. Intention: the perceived reason for why the speaker is giving the message.

Understanding these messages allows us to avoid pitfalls and pull people toward us. These messages are conveyed across multiple

---

[16] See, for example, Richards, I.A. and Ogden, C.K. *The Meaning of Meaning: A Study of the Influence of Language upon Thought and of the Science of Symbolism.* London and New York: Mariner Books, 1923.

channels. For example, we convey some of these messages with body language. Leaning backward with our arms crossed suggests that we are frustrated and not engaged. Leaning forward and focusing on your conversational partner lets them know that you are interested in what they have to say.

While our societal body of knowledge is found primarily in words, tone of voice and body language influence the message that you send each time you interact with someone else. What does this mean for you? It means that you can change the message you are sending by being cognizant of the reaction of others to what you do, say, and how you say it.

Innovative Questions and Our Messages

Remembering that it's important to accept emotions and provide a psychologically safe environment for the people with whom you interact, we suggest that you watch people's reactions to things that you say and do. Through practice, we can all become cognitively more aware of the message we are sending and how others are interpreting these messages. Then, if you feel a high-arousal emotional situation has occurred, you can assess the event with questions:

- I get the sense that what I am saying is upsetting you. Is that accurate?
- I'm getting the sense that you want to be argumentative right now. Is that accurate?
- Did what I said upset you?

Here's a pattern we suggest for understanding what's going on:

Make a statement.
Ask the question.
Shut up and listen.

If people disagree with the question you presented, you can respond with, "I'm just telling you how I interpret it. What do you think?" This allows for the conversation to drill down into the root cause of what's going on. Once you gain clarity on what's going on, you have a better opportunity to change how you are interacting with someone else. Remember the questions on *Stasis* in the fable? Clarity is power.

Story: Pushing and Pulling

John was talking to Sally about an incident that really upset him. One of John's team members just took credit for something that John did. He was hoping that Sally, his supervisor, would intervene. However, while he was telling his story, Sally was busy typing away at an e-mail, interjecting with an occasional nod or "uh-huh." John walked out of the room frustrated.

Sally clearly pushed John away in this example. Let's take a look how that same conversation could've gone differently:

John walked into Sally's office to talk about something that really upset him. Steve, another team member, just took credit for the new advertising campaign. John was completely aggravated. Sally stopped what she was doing and took a seat right next to John. She started asking clarifying questions, including the following (of course, waiting for an answer after each one). When did you find out about what Steve did? How do you know he took your idea? Have you talked to Steve directly? How were you hoping I could help you? Can I give you a suggestion? Do you want me to share with you how I would approach this if I were you?

In this scenario, Sally has helped build her relationship with John. She's also shown her willingness to help him solve the problem and make a decision that's in line with John's goals and intents. And, Sally did not do this only with words. She conveyed this with her actions, body language, and emotion.

Some other *Innovative Questions* that pull someone toward us include:

- What do you need more of? Less of? What do you need to start?
- What should stop so you can do your job better?
- Paraphrasing what you just heard and asking, "Is that accurate?"
- What were you hoping that I could do for you?

Allies

One of Chris's clients, Larry, was a senior partner in a large law firm. Larry excelled at pushing people away because he liked to show how smart he was and didn't seem to listen to other people.

When Chris started coaching Larry, he talked about how Larry needed more allies. Allies, Chris said, could help Larry achieve his goals and give feedback and suggestions to him when he wasn't being as effective as he could be at achieving his goals. Chris taught Larry some essential skills:

1. Look to find common ground.
2. Help people achieve their own goals.
3. Ask people what you can do to help.
4. Start with a small statement, and then ask a question.
5. Allow the people having the conflict with you to do the talking. Don't perform a monologue.
6. Ask the question, "Something is on my mind. Can I share it with you?"

In the end, Larry learned how to pull people toward him, and he became a lot more effective. At the end of his engagement with Chris, Larry had more allies than when he started. Larry became much more aware of the impact his behavior was having on others by testing assumptions and asking questions, fundamental tenets of IQs.

Summary

Innovative Questions help you pull people toward you, and that not only makes you a more effective leader, it makes your job more enjoyable, as people actually want to work with you. By learning this additional effective method of working with others, you will have one more dynamic tool in your arsenal.

Things You Can Do

- Instead of sitting behind your desk when you are talking to someone else, try sitting beside them.
- Try an *Innovative Question* from this chapter the next time you are dealing with an emotionally charged situation.
- Try feeding back what someone has said and then ask, "Is that accurate?"

CHAPTER 10

Assessing Readiness

If you recall from our introduction, David first met Chris at the UCLA Technical Management Program (TMP). At the TMP, students participate in four intensive management classes each day, each one two hours long. In David's last class of the day, David met Chris. Much to David's horror, Chris started his class by putting up a diagram that looked like the image on the following page.

David had already been through three two-hour classes that day, and he started thinking of ways he was going to skip this class for the rest of the week. How was he going to get anything out of four boxes? This was just going to be a class of management mumbo-jumbo, and he wasn't interested.

After the first class, David realized he was wrong.[17] He also realized that he was not managing his team as effectively as he could have, because he wasn't looking at the individual capabilities of his team to perform tasks in the most effective way.

---

[17] Frankly, David was captivated.

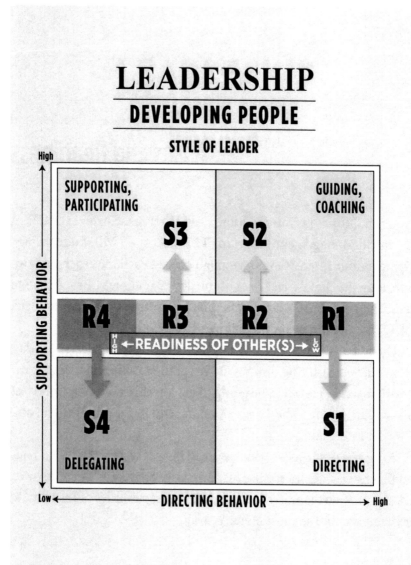

Figure 10.1: Assessing Readiness Diagram

Situational Leadership™

David was learning about a model referred to as Situational Leadership™[18]. Initially introduced by Paul Hersey and Ken Blanchard, Situational Leadership™ talks about effective ways that leaders can delegate tasks to others. Situational Leadership™ provides insight to the way we need to coach and mentor an individual on each task that they perform. How do we suggest you do this? You ask questions that help you understand at what level each person can operate on each task.

Assessing Readiness

Situational Leadership™ teaches us to assess the readiness of another to perform a particular task in a particular situation. Leaders must know how to effectively manage others in order to help them execute on an outcome. Since different individuals have different readiness levels when it comes to performing a particular task, combining IQs and assessing readiness allows individuals to more effectively lead their teams.

We call being able to successfully execute on a specific task *readiness*. Before tackling the definition of readiness, let's talk about tasks. A number of things must be in place to achieve a task:

- We must be clear on the task, meaning we define the *Ideal Final Result* (IFR) for that task in advance.
- We must agree on intermediate objectives.

---

[18] Hersey, P. and Blanchard, K. H., *Management of Organizational Behavior — Utilizing Human Resources,* New Jersey: Prentice Hall, 1969.

- We need to set deadlines.
- Finally, we have to contract for styles. This means that we have to agree on the way in which the manager and the team member are going to interact in getting a task done to achieve the objective (the *Ideal Final Result*).

Task Breakdown

Let's take a simple task and take a look at how it breaks down. Here's an example of creating an arbor in a garden. The following steps or tasks are required to finish the project and accomplish the objective:

- Draw the design
- Sign off on the design
- Create a scope of material
- Create a budget
- Value engineer the project within the budget
- Contract someone to build the arbor
- Establish milestones
- Sign off on the completed project

Each of these discrete tasks requires execution. And, here's the critical element: For each of these discrete tasks, an individual has a different *readiness* level for completing the task.

Readiness is a combination of ability and willingness. Someone can be perfectly able to do a particular task and not willing to do it at all. For example, with the arbor example, someone might be an accomplished carpenter and say that they are not willing to build the arbor during the summer because it's too hot or because they are just too busy at that time.

Ability

Let's take a further look at *ability* and *willingness*. *Ability* is made up of three different factors:

- Experience
- Training
- Understanding the competing priorities within the task

Ability can also be called the demonstrated ability to produce consistent results. *Ability* isn't very much good if the results are not consistent. This means that task-specific experience is critical to someone being *able* to get something done and get it done consistently. If someone has no experience whatsoever in performing something, it's not likely to be done well, consistently, or on time. Education and training also have a good deal to do with the *ability* to execute on a task, so long as the education is related to performing the task. Furthermore, understanding the priorities of particular elements of tasks helps people perform on their own without coaching because they can shift from one priority to another, depending on the situation.

Innovative Questions you can ask to assess someone's *ability* for a particular task include:

- Have you done this before?
- What were your successes the last time you did this task?
- What specific training have you had around this specific task?
- How do you prioritize different tasks?
- What do you see as the priority of this task compared to others?
- How do you think you might resolve the situation? What do you think is the best resolution?

- What resources do you think you might use in getting this done?
- Can you commit to getting to me in the event that you run into any issues?

Willingness

Willingness is the complement to *ability* in assessing *readiness*. *Willingness* is made up the following three factors:

- Confidence
- Desire
- Incentive

Confidence is the knowledge that someone will succeed. If they have done it before and done it repeatedly well, an individual will be confident that they can do it again. Desire is the intrinsic motivation to get something done, while incentive, such as a financial reward, is the extrinsic motivation to complete a task. The proof of *willingness* is "putting out the effort" to get something done.

Innovative Questions that help indicate that someone is *willing* to perform a task include:

- What are the benefits to you of getting this done? or What are the benefits of doing this?
- What's in it for you if you succeed in doing this? or What's in it for you if you perform this task?
- Do you want to do this task?
- Are you confident that this task can be achieved?
- On a scale of 1 to 10, how confident are you that you are capable of completing this project? or How confident are you that you will complete this project on time and on budget?

Now, add these two sets of questions to a final crucial point, and you have a truly strong formula for guiding others. Leaders need to assess the *readiness* of each individual, at a *particular* time, for each *situation-task* combination. Upon making this assessment, leaders need to determine an appropriate style with which to interact with that individual. As an analogy, when someone is born, they are not typically ready to do much more than eat and sleep. As human beings progress through their work life cycle, they are in different places with regard to what they are capable of and willing to do. While clarity is of critical importance, it does little good to have clarity in a situation when your resource is not *ready* to implement what needs to be done.

Additionally, exceptional managers and coaches help individuals shorten their learning curve by teaching skills or the ability to execute more quickly than they might have otherwise. As people progress through their *readiness* cycle for a particular task, managers can speed this process by choosing an appropriate style for each *readiness* level.

Story: Real Life Practice

One of the things we believe differentiates this book from other manuscripts created by consultants centers around the relationship between David and Chris. Like all of Chris's clients, David is Chris' student who has operationalized the theory and uses it on a day-to-day basis. We hope that makes the things we are discussing in the book real for you. Here's a story about David's journey in assessing *readiness*.

David did not immediately absorb the full impact of assessing *readiness* until well into writing the book. He learned about it in class with Chris, he worked on it on site with his team and Chris, and he continued to work on it as he consulted with Chris, having some very nice successes along the way. It wasn't until a Sunday-morning conversation discussing one of David's staff members that David finally understood the true power of the model. Chris said, "No, no, no. You have to assess *readiness* for each task each time. It changes all the time." The light bulb went on in David's head. David's journey helps us to present this operationalized model of assessing readiness in the diagram we present in the paragraph.

Readiness Diagram

With that in mind, here's a representation of our interpretation of Situational Leadership™:

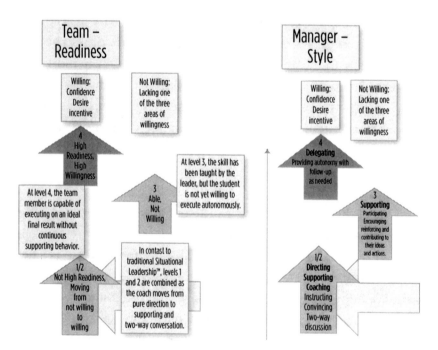

Figure 10.2: Situational Leadership™ Interpretation

Levels 1/2

Let's begin our discussion of this diagram moving from the bottom up. In Situational Leadership™, there are four different levels of readiness for each situation-task pairing. In our interpretation, we combine the first two levels into level 1/2. At this level, the leader/coach is instructing an individual on the elements of achieving a particular objective. The leader/coach is telling the team member what, where, when, and how. In other words, this is the part of coaching where a task is taught to another individual. The individual constantly receives instruction and supervision from the coach while progressing through the lower sub-levels of level 1/2.

At the lowest sub-levels of 1/2, individuals are not *willing* to perform the task. Typically, this is because they are not confident that they can perform the task and need to be told step-by-step how to do it.

We combine levels one and two because the difference between the two levels is defined by the interaction the leader/coach has with the team member. At the lowest sub-level of 1/2, the leader/coach is simply telling the team member what, where, when, and how. At the highest sub-level of 1/2, the leader/coach is engaging in a two-way conversation, helping the team member understand the "why" and become ready for the next level.

This interaction between *readiness* and managerial style is represented in our diagram between the two sides. For each level of *readiness* on the left side of the diagram, a complementary *style* exists on the right side of the diagram. *Readiness* level 1/2 is complemented by managerial *style* level 1/2. An individual at level 1/2 is minimally ready and willing to do the task, so we characterize this level by the manager explaining, demonstrating, and giving feedback on performance. The manager might say, "Let me explain this step by step. After that, I'll give you a chance to try your hand at it. Don't worry about learning everything at once, because I'll be here to provide any assistance you may need."

Hersey and Blanchard refer to this behavior as directing, because the manager takes the staff member through each task's part step by step, with as much detail as possible.

Another part of *readiness* level 1/2 style is the *support* that the manager gives to the team member. *Support* consists of setting positive expectations and providing enough two-way communication to ensure that directions are clear and feedback is understood. An IQ around *support* would be, "Are my instructions to you clear, and do you understand them?" Note that this question not only provides *support* to the team member, it also helps the leader assess whether the team member needs more direction or more *support*.

In this way, as an individual becomes more confident in level 1/2, the leader/coach can switch from pure direction and confirmation of understanding to more *support*. *Support* also refers to the way a leader/coach encourages and assists a team member. The leader/coach might say, "I appreciate your enthusiasm for this task. Let me explain why we do it this way, and then I'll answer any questions you have. We'll make sure you have what you need to do an excellent job."

Level 3

Level 3 is a significant transition from level 1/2. In this level, individuals learn how to perform a task on their own with the support of their leader/coach. As a result, level 3 creates a give-and-take collaboration between the leader/coach and the team member.

When using *style* 3, the leader does not "tell" or "direct" the other person. Instead, the leader shares responsibility for decision-making. IQs at this level might sound like, "Susan, we can all benefit from some of the approaches you have used in the past. How do you think we should proceed on this?" Alternatively, a manager might say, "What are your thoughts on how to do this?"

Level 4

Level 4 is another large step in the *readiness* matrix. In this level, the team member becomes in sync with the current manager. The team member now uses a common language to communicate with his or her manager and essentially becomes an extension of the manager[19]. This level is characterized by a more "hands-off" approach that gives the team member room to make and implement decisions. Of all the styles, style 4 is the least structured. An *Innovative Question* for style 4 might sound like this (note that this is actually a statement, confirmed with a question): "Jim, you know the results we are looking for. This project is right up your alley. Take responsibility; you know the parameters and the constraints. Call me if you need me. Are you okay with this?" The leader delegates the task to the team member and uses supporting behavior to reinforce and later reward the person for achieving intended results.

Shortcuts to Assessment

In order to effectively arrive at the *Ideal Final Result,* leaders need to decide what level of *readiness* an individual possesses for a particular task and then choose an appropriate *style* that matches the *readiness* level. A shortcut for deciding how you can best guide individuals can be achieved through the following series of IQs:

- How would you like me to interact with you on this assignment? or How can I be the most helpful? (Any level, depending on response)
- Would you like me to walk you through it? (level 1/2)
- Would you like me to make some suggestions about how I would do it? Would you like to ask me some questions and then have me give you feedback? (higher sub-levels of level 1/2)
- Would you like to bounce your ideas off of me? (level 3)

---

[19] This is not to say that the team member has to do everything exactly as the manager would. It means that the team member understands the requirements and constraints of the particular task and how to achieve the *Ideal Final Result.*

- Would you like to run with this on your own and get to me if you need me? (level 4)

By listening to the responses to each of these questions, you can quickly gauge at which level an individual rests for each particular task.

In going through these questions, you will also sense from time to time that individuals are not ready or willing to do the task or project. Here are some questions you can ask in these situations:

- I'm sensing that you are reluctant to do this project. or I'm sensing that you are reluctant to run with this project on your own. Is that an accurate statement?
- You seem to be uneasy about completing this project. Can you tell me if that's true?

Depending on the response to these questions, you can alter the style with which you engage your staff members.

Clarity

As managers move through the levels of this model, initial clarity becomes more and more critical. A manager who has delegated a task and allows individuals to work autonomously (level 4) does not have the luxury, if you can call it that, of repeatedly intervening and correcting course when the *Ideal Final Result* is not accurately defined in the first place. This leads to a downward spiral of frustration all around. In order for clarity to provide power, it most definitely needs to be defined upfront.

Story: Managing a Project

Here's an example of how assessing readiness provides a framework for measuring how you as a manager can best interact with each of your staff members on a task-by-task basis. In working with your staff members, altering your style appropriately provides for the most productive outcomes for each individual.

Dan is taking on his first significant project. He's going to run a patch-management software upgrade to an important system for the company and is very concerned about each step he is going to need to take. He is worried he will make a mistake that will make him and his team look bad. His manager, Susan, decides that, initially, he will need to be directed on the right steps for the software upgrade to be successful and then coached through the actual process of managing a small team of people who are going to apply patches to the server.

Initially, Dan has no idea what to do, so, since he does not have previous experience on this particular task, we would say he has low *readiness*. Furthermore, while he wants to take on the task, he is not confident that he can complete it well, so, we would say his confidence is low and that his low confidence will affect his willingness. Because of both low *ability* and *willingness*, he initially needs to be directed on each individual step.

After he has completed the task successfully, most likely multiple times, he will be ready to move on to level 3 and work under the guidance of his leader/coach, Susan. At this level, he will be instigating the decisions, but he will still have a coach at his side with whom he can bounce his ideas around.

Additional IQs and *Readiness*

In summary, depending on an individual's *readiness* level, a leader can vary the questions used in their interactions to best support their team member. It's important to remember that *readiness* is task specific. Being *ready* for one task does not equate to being *ready* for another. Given that different people need different help in arriving at the *Ideal Final Result* and in reporting back to you as a manager, let's take a look at a few more IQs to use for each *readiness* level:

Level 1/2

Individuals at level 1/2 need clear step-by-step instructions and appropriate support. Some appropriate questions are:

- What questions do you have for me?
- Just to make sure we are on the same page — are you comfortable with coming to me after each task is completed?
- Do you understand that, if you do not understand my instructions at any time, you need to get to me right away?
- Do you have any thoughts about what we just discussed?
- Can I give you any more information to help you succeed?
- Are we agreed on the outcome?

Level 3

Here are some questions that can help you in appropriately supporting someone who is preparing to fly on their own:

- How do you plan on completing this project on time and on budget?
- What do you need from me?
- What needs to start/stop in order to allow you to make this happen?
- I want to reiterate that you will get to me if there is a problem. Are you clear on that?
- What types of ideas do you have for getting this project done?
- What type of support would you like to have from me to get this project done?

Level 4

At level 4, you will want to give your team member the largest amount of freedom that you possibly can. This team member possesses both *ability* and *willingness*. They have a proven track record of consistent successful execution (experience), they have had appropriate training, and they understand how to manage priorities as they change. They are also confident in their ability to execute, and they have a desire and an incentive to do the task. Questions you might want to use include:

- What is our *Ideal Final Result*?
- What is your plan?
- How do you want to check in with me?
- Do you need anything from me?

Individuals at level 4 are capable of running with the ball on their own for a specific task, so they deserve a defined outcome and the space to do their job well.

Re-assessing *Readiness*

As we're talking about *readiness*, we want you to remember that you may not initially assess an individual's *readiness* level correctly. Their *readiness* may also change over time or with different circumstances. If you find that your team member is not at the *readiness* level you thought they were, then your team member is either not *able* or not *willing* to operate at the level at which you are communicating to them. *Innovative Questions* are all about drilling down and finding what's really going on. In these cases, we suggest you go back to our shortcut questions for assessing readiness to help you find the particular sticking or *Stasis* point.

Summary

In closing, *readiness* assessment allows leaders to pick the right type of style and questions to ask to most appropriately guide and mentor their team members. Remember, though, to make this a fluid assessment process. *Readiness* changes all the time. We want to leave you with this one thought — If you do find that individuals are stuck on a particular point, and you can't get past it, you can always ask another IQ. Here are some of our most effective questions that help you get past the *Stasis* points:

- Could the opposite of what you just said be true? (One of our favorites!)
- Correct me if I am wrong, but are we not in agreement on this?
- I know you think this has not worked in the past. If you could wave a magic wand and make all of those problems disappear, how would you do it?
- I know you think this has not worked in the past. What if all of those political, budgetary, and other problems were erased? How would you make this happen?
- What part of what I just said do you agree with?
- If you were me, what would you do differently?

CHAPTER 11

Change Management

As you begin to implement our suggestions from this book, we want to convey the importance of telling your teams that you are working on your leadership behaviors and, more specifically, on which skills you are working to improve. For example, after his workshop at UCLA on Leadership Styles for Infuencing Others, David began consciously assessing individuals' readiness and attempting to modify his style appropriately. Unfortunately, in his overzealousness, he did this without talking to his team about it. First, the team had no idea what David was trying to do. Second, they were simply confused by the new language.

Because he didn't take the time to explain what he was doing upfront, David lost the opportunity to create a common language with his team. Realizing the error of his ways, David subsequently explained the model to his team and also brought Chris in to help facilitate an understanding of the model. Now team members regularly say, "You're giving me too much Style 1 (you're being too directive) so 'back off.'" Or, "I'm feeling that I'm not going to complete this task on time; can I please get some additional guidance?" Having a common language so people can speak about being ready, capable, and willing provides a very powerful conduit to success.

Having everyone on board with the changes that you are making allows for people to bloom, grow, and get better at what they do. Most importantly, it doesn't work nearly as effectively unless everyone understands the model and the language. This chapter is about how to communicate your change.

Being Upfront About Change

As we discussed in our chapter on personal change, change is hard. It's even harder, sometimes, for those people around you. As a leader, while you are trying to change, others need to know that you are making changes as well. One of the most powerful tools you can use is to be upfront about the fact that you are trying to change. As you work through the inevitable turmoil and foibles of making changes, your success depends not only on what you do, it also depends on how others react to you.

If you recall from our chapter on change, one of Chris's clients stood up in front of his entire leadership team and apologized for his past behavior. This let people know that he was trying to change and it started to lay the foundation for people to accept the specific change he committed to. When someone stands up in front of a crowd and admits to being wrong, that makes people pay attention to what's going on and think that the possibility for change exists. Opening this space is a critical step in being effective.

Repeatedly talking about the changes you are trying to make also helps people assimilate in their minds the change you are making. Individuals have already put you in a particular box, and it will help them to know that you are trying to change. Telling them what and how you are trying to change lets them measure your success. And, since people don't tend to change perceptions quickly, reminding them along the way is critical.

Asking About Change

Here is a simple way to convey that you are working on a change. It doesn't need to take more than a minute or two. You can start out by saying something like, "As you know, Jim, I have committed to becoming more effective at collaborating with others and listening to different points of view with an open mind. In the last month or so, have you noticed a difference?" Then, shut up, listen, and say, "Thank you" for any feedback. You should also ask, "Is there anything specific you can point to?" and "Do you have any specific suggestions for me moving forward?" Asking these questions not only sends the message that you are changing and want feedback and suggestions, it also allows you to incorporate this feedback to better make your change.

Apologizing

Apologizing for slipping up is another good way of letting your team know that you are making a change and reminding yourself and others that you are committed to making that change. Disarming angry people with an apology can be a very strong tool in your change arsenal.

There are a number of aspects of the apology that are important in our dialogue. The first deals with the leader as a learner too, which shows his or her vulnerability to the team. Letting them know that you make mistakes shows you as human and willing to admit when you are wrong. Also, making an apology earnestly expresses a desire to improve. For example, you might say:

> I'm sorry; I was wrong. What can I do to make it right? I will do my very best not to do that again. Will you please forgive me?

Innovative Questions center on the tenet that the manager has honor. Acting honorably includes owning up to one's mistakes. A manager, particularly one who is trying out new things, is going to make mistakes. Publicly admitting to these mistakes shows that the manager is human and honorable. Simply saying, "I know I've been working on being less sarcastic, and I am sorry I slipped. I'll work hard for that not to happen again," goes a very long way with team members.

Patience

In changing behaviors, you also need to be patient. You can't expect people to change their perception of you or their interactions with you because you've changed for a few weeks. Give it some time, and you will start seeing some results.

Chris once worked with Brad, a client who was in a conflict with two of his peers. One of the peers was willing to give Brad a chance and had an open mind. The other had already decided Brad wasn't going to change. Over time, the manager with the open mind won over the manager who wouldn't look at Brad differently. However, because Brad worked hard on communicating change, eventually the change was made and processed by his peers.

Summary

You must communicate changes to those around you. People have already put you in a box and decided what you are about. You can change this, and you are taking the first step by reading this book and starting to make changes in the way you interact with others.

Things You Can Do

- Clearly and specifically define the changes you are making to your team members and peers.
- Ask others for feedback on how you are doing.
- Remind yourself and others that you are human by apologizing when you slip up on the behaviors you are trying to change.

CHAPTER 12

Nonnegotiables and Communication

Every manager has a set of negotiable and *nonnegotiable* rules that must be communicated to their teams. While we are clearly huge advocates of asking questions, in some cases it's necessary to set expectations or ground rules. We have spent a reasonable amount of time talking about honor and integrity with regard to dealing with other humans. These are certainly important ground rules to build with your team, and your team must know that they need to follow the same rules as you do.

Critical Ground Rules

In this chapter, we specifically identify some critical ground rules of communication between individuals and how to go about communicating them. Managers must communicate the expectations of getting to him or her, as well as stakeholders, before it is too late to correct course or fix a problem. Many leaders have made the mistake of assuming that a team member will get to them when there is a problem, and when they don't do that in a timely manner, severe consequences can arise. We urge leaders to make this clear upfront. *Innovative Questions* fail miserably when people don't know that they need to communicate with others.

Explanations

Explaining the background of a *nonnegotiable* requirement is the most important element of communicating your expectations. Explaining why you ask for a particular *nonnegotiable* requirement helps someone understand the reason behind a particular ground rule and makes it more likely that they will support you in that requirement. An explanation of a *nonnegotiable* ground rule also helps those you coach understand why certain things are important in general and why they are important to you.

One Nonnegotiable Example

One example of a nonnegotiable is helping people understand how they are responsible for keeping both spoken and unspoken commitments to those with whom they interact (see figure 12.1):

Responsible Interactions

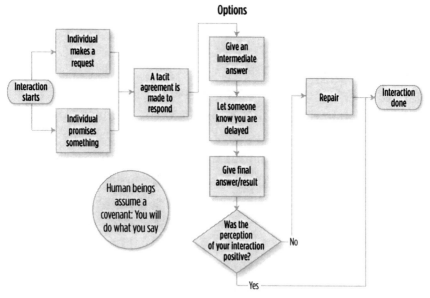

Figure 12.1

In this diagram, we show how individuals have an unspoken agreement to follow up. Not only does the manager compel a staff member to follow up with him or her, on any given project, there are numerous stakeholders who need to be kept in the loop. As simple a concept as this may be to a manager, many projects run into problems because team members do not adhere to this requirement.

Explaining the importance of this concept to your team has multiple benefits. By keeping people in the loop, problems can be resolved sooner. Because problems are put on the table when they arise, they don't fester and get worse. Understanding responsible interactions helps your team members understand the benefit to them of acting this way, the benefit to those they interact with, and the benefit to you. Expressing this concept upfront as a ground rule also helps your team understand your expectations of them.

Getting to Your Bosses

In the following diagram, we further clarify this responsibility. Managers cannot manage effectively if their staff members are not keeping them informed. And, stakeholders will not be happy if they are not updated as their projects proceed. In particular, if there is something going wrong with a project, the manager or stakeholder needs to know right away. And, again, while this may seem like a simple concept, it's one that gets in the way of business every day (see figure 12.2).

We cannot emphasize enough the criticality of collaboration between project managers and their direct managers. Managers have access to resources and are privy to information to which their direct reports do not have access. Managers who are empowering their staffs need to be brought into the loop when things are not going according to expectation. And, as an effective manager, you absolutely need to communicate this expectation upfront.

Update Loop

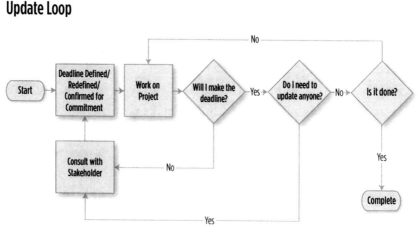

Figure 12.2

Summary

Making sure that communication occurs in between interactions between individuals is a critical tenet to the success of IQs. Managers must make sure that these *nonnegotiable* communication requirements are defined. Furthermore, since many other ground rules exist that are important to particular managers and teams, each manager should assess what these ground rules are and make sure they are clearly communicated to their team.

Things You Can Do

- State what your negotiable and *nonnegotiable* ground rules are upfront. For example, David uses a ground-rules chart that he created with his team.
- Explain in detail why you have a particular nonnegotiable requirement and discuss negotiable ground rules.
- Make sure getting to you and other stakeholders when there is a problem is a clear expectation.

CHAPTER 13

After Action Review

Once a team completes a task, some of the most important work has yet to be done. We call this the After Action Review, and it presents a great opportunity for doing even better next time. As with all *Innovative Questions* and *Space Creation,* the After Action Review centers on asking questions.

An After Action Review allows you and your team to get better all the time and is comprised of five key questions:

1. What did you set out to do?
2. What actually happened?
3. How did it happen?
4. What insights do you have?
5. What are you going to do moving forward? or
6. If you could do it again, what would you repeat and what would you do differently?

Each of these questions focuses on a specific non-judgmental topic with the purpose of gleaning information from your team members and having them draw their own conclusions without eliciting a preprogrammed defensive reaction. Instead, these questions create

Safe Space for thoughtful consideration. Let's take a look at these IQs one by one.

The first question, "What did you set out to do?" allows the individual to truly think about what they intended as the outcome. An After Action Review should start from an objective perspective of what the initial goal was, not a point of blame. This first question also asks them to retrospectively think about whether they properly defined their *Ideal Final Result* upfront. This provides a valuable learning lesson for next time without injecting judgment into the equation.

In assessing what actually happened (the second question), the individual is comparing this reality to both their initial and revised *Ideal Final Results*. It blends wonderfully with the third question, "How did the project unfold?" with regard to both your expectations as well as everyone else's involved in the project. It asks your mind to make a comparison of what could have been better versus what happened according to plan and what the unintended consequences were.

Note that, in question number three, we use "how did it happen?" instead of "why did it happen?" or "who is responsible?" "Why" implies blame, and that doesn't necessarily lead to clarity; it often leads to an argument. "How" allows for the brain to effectively replay what happened and process through a series of questions that clarifies what could be better. This is another example of how words have meanings and how little changes can make a big difference.

The next two questions focus on individual insights: "What did *you* learn?" and, "What would *you* do differently next time?" Because we stay away from thoughts like, "How could you let this happen?" "What went wrong?" and "Who is responsible?" we open up the brain to more possibilities and to self-learning. We also allow individuals the opportunity to come to their own conclusions, which leads to *getting it*, an important point we discussed previously. When individuals get it, they are truly learning, and they apply that learning in their next project or interaction.

Little After Action Reviews

Chris often suggests to his leaders that they use the After Action Review on smaller items as well. For example, after each meeting, he suggests that they go through the five questions and see whether or not they actually accomplished their goal or goals for the meeting. Perhaps they might be able to see whether the meeting was necessary at all or if there was another, more efficient way to arrive at the goal for the meeting. If you find that meetings are primarily informational, there is probably a more effective way to disseminate the information and ensure that meetings are instead used to advance decision-making.

This ability to do After Action Reviews also applies to your interactions with others. Ask yourself the six questions with every interaction you have. See if this technique can help you get better in everything you do.

Conclusion

Innovative Questions are a highly effective way to assess what has happened, what is going on right now, and what might happen next. By applying *Innovative Questions* in an After Action Review, you and your team can expand the way your minds normally process a problem, growing the potential for improvement. Furthermore, by suggesting to your team that they run through these questions on their own and together, you are all learning to get better all the time. Finally, as your team members are aware they will be asked these questions, they will tend to come to each meeting and interaction more prepared. Because they are habitually thinking about how to get better, they will begin doing these reviews automatically.

Things You Can Do

- Begin doing after action reviews after each project.
- Conduct after action reviews for smaller tasks or meetings.
- Think about the language you use when you ask how something went the way it did.

Turning It Around

We've all experienced it. You have a conflict with another individual, and you are getting nowhere. They are mad. You are mad. They keep saying the same thing, and you keep saying the same thing. You just can't seem to find a resolution.

Most of us find conversations involving conflict uncomfortable. Even worse, when two individuals are doing a dance in which they don't even hear each other and they can't get to any sort of resolution, the interaction is simply not productive. The outcomes aren't positive, the process doesn't feel good, and people walk away from the table feeling upset and hurt. It doesn't have to be this way. *Innovative Questions* allow us to turn these negative situations around.

Four Examples

In order to show you how this works, let's start by looking at some options in normally difficult situations:

Problem	*Innovative Question* to ask
An individual will not even consider your idea.	I am getting the sense that your mind is made up and new information won't matter. Is that accurate?
An individual agrees on the end result but doesn't like the path you or a team member proposes.	You and I agree on the desired result, and I am right in line with you on your first two steps. I have difficulty seeing how your third and fourth steps get us to where we want to be. What am I missing?
An individual appears upset with you. You don't necessarily see why he or she is upset, but you'd like to smooth the waters.	Whatever part I had in creating this rift, please accept my apology. It was not my intention. What would you like me to do more of or less of?
You see that someone is not in a particularly accepting mood for new ideas.	Get them to say, "Yes." Ask them, "Can I offer a suggestion?"

With each of these questions, the phrasings stop people in their tracks, make them think, and reset the conversational path. Let's break down the first question, "I am getting the sense that your mind is made up. Is that accurate?" We first make a statement and ask the person to respond to it. First, this statement/question pattern forces the individual to think about what we said — whether or not his or her mind is, in reality, closed to what we are saying. Second, it stops the habitual response and makes them actually think about what they are saying by asking them to respond to the question.

With the second question, we start by setting up that we agree on the desired results (finding common ground), and we also point out where we are in agreement on the tactics to get there. We also state where we are not in agreement and give our partner the opportunity to convince us by asking the question "What am I missing?" It sets the stage by showing that you are willing to listen to what they have to say.

In the third question, "Whatever part I had in creating this rift, please accept my apology," we apologize to our conversational partner. This technique works only if you come across as sincere (and we hope you are truly sincere). This often takes the wind out of the angry sails of your conversation. The outcome can be quite surprising and positive. Because we follow up this apology with asking what you can do to make it better in terms of voluntary behavior, the person once again can see good interests at work.

Finally, in the fourth example, we ask the simple question, "Can I offer a suggestion?" Instead of simply inserting your belief, you ask the person to give you permission to make a suggestion. We have found, and the research supports our anecdotal findings that people are much more likely to listen to and consider a suggestion once they have given you permission to make one.

Intent and Tone

Your intent and tone while questioning is very important because people can get petulant and angry when you ask them questions they can't immediately answer, especially if they feel you are looking to embarrass them or make yourself look better. Be careful how you come across. As we've mentioned throughout this book, integrity and intention are both critical in being successful with *Innovative Questions*. Others are always observing, analyzing, and making judgments on *your* integrity and intention. If you truly have the best interest of an individual in mind and are a fair player, you will end up with more outstanding outcomes.

Tactical Formulas

In order to drive home the concepts behind *Innovative Questions*, here are some formulas to apply in each of your interactions. For confrontational situations specifically, we suggest that you follow one or more of the following tactics:

- Make a statement and then ask, "Would you agree?"
- Ask a question or make a statement to follow up. For example, "Help me understand what _____ means."
- Probe further by directly confronting any resistance you feel. For example, "I get the sense that you are not completely on board with what I'm talking about. Is that accurate?"
- Listen, don't argue, and then paraphrase back your understanding of what the person has said when they have finished. Remember, you're not trying to win a debate or recite a monologue to convince them they are wrong. You want to achieve the best possible outcome.
- Use a question that turns around whatever the individual is saying, and ask them to reconsider. Our favorite is, "Is it possible that the opposite of what you are saying is true?" Appendix C is chock-full of just such questions that you can select for the appropriate situation.

We will put these formulas into action a bit later in the chapter.

Common Ground

The search for an outcome proceeds most effectively when we seek to find common ground. We suggest you begin, as you might have guessed, by asking a few questions. "What can we agree on with respect to what we just discussed?" "Let's list out where we have similar points of views." "Can we find a common denominator within what we are discussing?"

As we previously discussed, research has shown that finding a common denominator is better than a compromise. With a compromise, both parties can feel they lost. With a common denominator, there is some winning for everyone. Of course, a win-win provides the best solution, but win-win cannot always be achieved. By asking, "What do we both need for this to happen?" people think about both sides, rather than just their own needs. If everyone can walk away from the table with a win, even a little one, the chances increase for everyone to walk away satisfied. When people walk away satisfied, you avoid the dark alternative where they immediately start to undermine the decision, so that, later on, they can say, "I told you so."

Consensus

Our clients and leaders have often asked about consensus. Individuals throw around the word "consensus" rather loosely, so it's important to get clarity on what you are talking about. Does consensus mean the leader won't leave the room until everyone agrees with him? Have you achieved consensus when the majority agrees? Does it need to be 70%? Perhaps even more importantly, would the leader be willing to surrender his or her position power and let the group achieve consensus even if he or she does not agree? We addressed consensus in our fable, *The Storm and the Calm*, and want to reiterate that achieving clarity on how consensus will work before beginning the conversation helps smooth the way to a good resolution and understanding what consensus means in decision-making for your team.

Disagreements

During a conversation, you will almost inevitably disagree with something that someone else says. You could say, "I disagree with you," and disrupt the flow of the meeting. Or, you could ask clarifying questions. Some examples are, "Could you please define that for me?" Or, "Can you help me understand that point of view?"

Some other things you can say when you disagree include:

That's interesting. Can I ask you a couple of questions? My understanding was something different.

You make a statement, and someone says, "I don't think that's true." In response, you say, "Maybe you're correct; maybe it's not true. But if it is true, would you be willing to change your mind or at least reconsider your point of view?"

Someone is advocating for a certain policy. You can respond with, "Obviously, you're a big supporter of this cause. Can you give me a specific issue pertaining to this cause that you'd like to discuss that you feel strongly about? What about this specific item resonates with you?"

Give me an example of what you would like to see more of and less of. How do you think that would affect the outcome?

Remember, some of these statements and questions aren't all that different from what you may have used in the past. However, by simply changing a few words or turning something into a question, you have a much better chance of turning a negative situation into a positive one.

Taboo Statements

We'd like to take a moment and point out a few sentences that can aggravate a situation. As we've discussed repeatedly, words have meanings, and some of them are to be avoided. For example, when someone says "I'm confused," they almost always mean "I disagree." We want you to avoid the term "I'm confused." We culturally understand that this phrase has a negative connotation, so we suggest you try another way of gaining clarity. You might respond by saying, "I'd like to get clearer on that. Can you explain it to me?" or "Help me understand what you are trying to say."

On the other hand, someone might disagree with you but not feel comfortable putting that directly on the table. If they say to you, "I'm confused," you can respond with a question that opens the dialogue. You might say, "Are you actually confused, or do you disagree?" Depending on the answer, you can either help them understand what's really going on and/or work to a common understanding of where you disagree and move to a solution from there.

As we will show shortly, and fairly obviously, you should also avoid accusing and demanding statements. Instead, turn the conversation around and ask IQs.

Encouragement

It may sound self-evident, but stakeholders (those affected by the person changing) need to encourage people when they are changing. Saying things like, "I appreciate your openness" or "I appreciate how this conversation is going" can go a long way to reinforce positive change. If you happen to be in a position where you can influence others, saying something like, "You should really encourage John when he is trying to change" can go a long way toward helping someone to change for the better.

Leaders should be especially cognizant of encouraging those around them when their behavior changes. Saying things like, "I really appreciate how open you are being" or "Great job on thinking outside the box," "I've noticed you stating your point of view more strongly," or "I've noticed you deferring to other people's point of view more often, and I think that's terrific," can effectively help people as they work with you through *Innovative Questions*.

The Stonewall

> *There was no finding common ground with April these days. Every project was at the last minute, and she would never compromise on the outcome. Every time the conversation began about needing to be flexible in order to achieve goals, it ended up in the same vicious cycle of finger-pointing and stonewalling.*

Sound familiar? Someone conveys that they are incapable of solving a problem, either at all or in a way that is fair to all parties. Parents find this infuriating. Managers find it untenable. How do you address this? When someone says, "I don't think I can do that," you can respond in several ways. First, you can use a traditional *Innovative Question* to try to turn the process around. In this case, we like the "magic wand" question: "If you could wave a magic wand and make the situation better, what would you do?"

While, on the surface, the magic wand question might seem silly, it is actually incredibly effective. Repeatedly, David has used this question, and it stops people in their tracks. We'll take a look at a case study in which David actually used the magic wand question in practice a little bit later in this chapter.

If the magic wand question or a similar query doesn't work, possibly because a person appears to be stuck in a deep cycle of negativity, you can take a more risky approach and break up this pattern by saying, "I am certain that you can prove yourself right" and following up with "I hear you telling me that you cannot do this. I'm certain that you can make that a self-fulfilling prophecy." By stirring the pot in this way, you make people carefully think about what they are saying. We'd like to point out that this is a second resort, and you should always try an *Innovative Question* first.

In the case where someone doesn't want to take the bait on one of these items, you can also turn the tables on them. You might say, "I don't want to fight you on this. What are you doing to improve?" or "What do you think you should do to improve?" People don't like to show that they are stuck in a rut, so they will start to think about what they might do to improve on their own. And, even if they make up an imaginary story about what they have accomplished in the past, they are at least setting themselves up for a different course going forward.

If someone clearly bristles at your suggestion to do something, you can also try "I get the sense that this doesn't interest you. Is that an accurate assessment?" Or, alternatively, "On a scale of 1 to 10, how reluctant are you to implement my suggestion?" At the very least, even if you don't effect change right now, you will have some better insight into what's going on. If you recall from our chapter on assessing *readiness*, understanding specifically how to interact with others can help you as you coach and lead them.

The Confronter

Although confrontation tends to make many people uncomfortable, some people seem to thrive on confrontation. If you feel that someone is being confrontational and would like to stop them in their tracks, we have some *Innovative Question* options. You can defuse someone who just wants to argue by agreeing with him. For example, you might say, "I absolutely agree with you on that point. Can you tell me how you get from there to here?" This way, you change their focus from problem to solution and set them on a constructive path. The same concept of solution focus applies by asking a simple question before getting into a disagreement. You might ask, "What did I just say that we can agree on?"

If these less controversy-provoking questions don't work, you can try, "I'm getting the sense you are being confrontational. Is that an accurate assessment?" Since this question is rather abrupt, you will likely get some pushback from your conversational partner. They might say, "Well, that's a pretty personal question. I take offense to that." We'd like to suggest some answers. One option: "I'm just sharing my assessment of what's going on." If they tell you they aren't angry or being confrontational, you can follow up with, "Let me ask you a question, right now. Are you angry?" Or, you might ask, "What are you feeling right now" If you can't seem to get through to them, you can tell them your statements are based on your perspective. Try, for example, "Let me tell you how you are coming across to me right now."

In the event of someone not agreeing with your assessment, you can say, "To me, everything boils down to performance." You can then move on to discuss their impact on others. "The way you express yourself inhibits other people from participating in the process. I'd like to ask you not to do that. And, if you can't control this behavior, I will confront you on it." Remember, *Innovative Questions* aren't a panacea. Sometimes you need to state your nonnegotiable positions.

Expectations

In the previous chapter, we discussed the need for a manager to set ground rules, specifically related to communication. In difficult situations, sometimes you will need to address ground rules more directly than you might if you were starting from scratch with your team. Additionally, you may find yourself expressing ground rules that you think are common sense, like, as we will explore in just a moment, "yelling at your teammates in a meeting is not appropriate." Here are some suggestions that we have found to be effective:

- Let me be clear: here are my expectations.
- Let me give you the reasons I think you should do this.
- On this team, these are the norms by which we operate. Would you like to discuss them? Is there anything you'd like to add to these?

Story: The Angry Young Man

Let's take a look at a case study where one of David's staff verbally attacked other staff members during a meeting. The first conversation occurred before *Innovative Questions* were applied. Afterwards, we examine how *Innovative Questions* changed the entire flow and outcome of the conversation.

As you can see from the following dialogue, the initial conversation doesn't go so well:

David: I'm extremely disappointed with your behavior in our most recent staff meeting. It's completely unacceptable to attack others during that type of meeting.

Adam: I wasn't attacking anyone.

David: I completely disagree with you. Your comment that the process for installing our new technology was complete "crap" was inappropriate and completely unacceptable.

Adam: You know, you're always picking on me. You play favorites with John, and I'm held to a different standard.

This conversation went on and on (in a circle) for some time and did not come to a fruitful resolution. Let's examine what's going on in this initial dialogue. First, Adam immediately became defensive. His defense showed that he did not even understand where David was coming from. Even if people can see another perspective, which was a difficult thing for Adam to do, they often have a defensive reaction when challenged with statements that attack their behavior.

Additionally, David was not coming from a forward-looking, solution-oriented perspective but rather from a condemning, person-focused perspective, immediately creating a hostile conversation.

Rather than asking questions, David started the meeting off with an attack, saying, "I'm extremely disappointed with your behavior." When Adam countered, as would generally be expected, David said, "I completely disagree." The conversation was going nowhere before it even started.

After a coaching session with Chris, the entire demeanor of the conversation changed. Here's the technique that Chris taught David:

- Express what you know and the information you have.
- Let the other person know that you're concerned about the situation you are discussing.
- Do not pass judgment until the other person has spoken and given you their point of view.
- Strive for clarity over agreement. Clarity is power.

Here's how David, through the use of *Innovative Questions*, turned the conversation around the next time David and Adam met.

David: In our last staff meeting, you were very agitated. We talked about it the last time we met, and I was obviously concerned about what happened. I thought you might have some additional perspective, having had a bit of time between that conversation and now. Can we revisit what happened in that meeting?

Adam: Well, for the first thing, I wasn't agitated, as you indicated in the last meeting.

David: Okay, let's explore that further so I can understand where you're coming from. Let me ask another question. I heard you say that the process for installing our new technology was complete "crap." Is that an accurate statement?

Adam: Yes, that's true. What's your concern?

David: Do you think that the networking team might have been upset by your comment? That they might have felt you were demeaning them?

Adam: Well, actually, no.

David: I'm hearing you say that you don't think you came across as angry or agitated and calling the work "crap" was not demeaning? Is that accurate?

Adam: Yes, I was not angry.

David: Well, I've spoken to a couple of members of the team, and they felt upset about your outburst and found your comments belittling.

Adam: Are you saying there was something wrong with what I was saying about the outcome of the project?

David: Not necessarily. I'm proposing that your choice of words, tone of voice, and visible disdain for their work was received as hurtful to the team.

Adam: And, I'm saying in return that there was nothing wrong with what I said.

David: Well, let me point out the following to you. That type of behavior, including choice of words and tone of voice, is not

acceptable on my team. Are we clear? What can be done to
make sure this doesn't happen again?

Adam: You are always picking on me. You play favorites with John,
and I'm held to a different standard.

David: What evidence do you have to support what you're saying
right now?

Adam: Well, I didn't come prepared to discuss that right now.

David: Okay, so in the absence of any evidence to support your claim,
let me ask you a question. Is it possible that the opposite of
what you're saying is true?

Adam: What? (Adam has difficulty processing the new concept.)

David: Is it possible that the opposite of what you're saying is true,
that I've actually been more lenient on you than I have been
on John?

Adam: I don't think so. While that may be accurate in some situations, it absolutely is not what happened here.

David: I hear what you are saying, and I see we don't fully agree. Let
me leave you to think about that, and let's specifically delve
into what's going on here. What's going on that caused this
situation to arise, and what could you be doing differently?

Adam: (Thinks for a minute.) Well, I've been very frustrated with
the way the networking group has interacted with my team.

Adam has finally found a moment of clarity. How did this happen?
By changing the modality of the interaction, David created a space for
a more productive outcome. Instead of becoming a defensive, circular

conversation, the discussion moved forward toward the root cause of the problem. Once that was identified, the conversation could now focus on solutions. Let's take a moment to explore why focusing on solutions changes the outcome of the conversation.

The brain works by telling the neurons and synapses to focus on that which we tell it we tell it to focus. If we focus on the problem, we only see the problem. Not only that, it's easier for most people to focus on problems. One purpose of IQs: Focus on solutions.

David did not take the bait when Adam attempted to reframe the discussion to David's favoritism of John. David instead asked a follow-up question: "What evidence do you have to support what you're saying right now?" This question made Adam uncomfortable because Adam had no evidence to back up his position. And, as the answer showed, he knew it. David was able, using IQ techniques, to keep the conversation on a solution-based track and keep it from devolving off point.

Using *Innovative Questions* helps individuals get to a solution quicker than in usual situations, making conversations less contentious and more productive, because with an *Innovative Question*, the brain is focusing on solutions, not finding out why it couldn't get to one.[20]

As this conversation continued, the causes were further explored, and a solution-oriented approach continued:

David: Let's talk about your frustration with this process. What can you change to make this better?

Adam: Well, there's nothing I can do about it.

---

[20] We don't want to oversimplify this. Finding the root cause ensures that you identify the right cause of an issue so that particular problem doesn't happen again. Solving a problem quickly in a crisis without solving it properly just leaves the problem open to happening again. Individuals must execute with care and not gloss over finding a solution to the root cause just because one particular solution arises in the heat of the moment. Finding the *Ideal Final Result* continues to be the goal.

David: If you don't think you can do anything about it, I'm quite sure you can prove yourself to be right.

Adam: (Pauses, because he doesn't want to be wrong.) But I can't do anything about it.

David: So what I'm hearing you say is you don't have the ability to control anything about the situation. Is that correct?

Adam: That's right! I do not have the power to control what happened with the network group.

David: Do you think that you have the ability to influence the decision?

Adam: I'm not sure.

David: Okay. I believe you are seen by this group as a subject-matter expert with a lot of expertise in this process. Do you agree?

Adam (Pauses) I think so.

David I agree. Now, if you could wave a magic wand and change anything about this process, define what you wanted to see start and what you wanted to see stop, what would you do?

Adam: (Pauses. He is carefully thinking about it now.) When we have any new projects affecting my unit, I would like to make it mandatory that I sign off before the project starts.

As you can see, the conversation has taken a completely different turn. By challenging Adam with questions that are not part of the usual dance, we have helped him get out of his box and to see things differently. By creating *Safe Space*, David found out that Adam simply wanted to be consulted before decisions were made that affected him. In turn, David immediately implemented this easy solution with his team.

Closing

It's important that your team members understand that "no" and "never" are not options and that they can think through problems. In order to drive this point home, we want to encourage you to reinforce learning moments. Here's an example of what you can say:

Before we break, I want to revisit what just happened. You initially told me that you are powerless to make the changes that were needed to resolve this issue. You said, "It couldn't be done by you." Do you remember what I asked you?

I want to point out to you that you were able to resolve the issue by thinking differently, building a case, connecting the dots effectively, and articulating it well. I expect you to be capable of thinking beyond that which you see as a roadblock. I also think that this will be a very important skill for you to have in your arsenal. Remember: We control only our behavior and, to some extent, our thinking process. Effectively bringing these to a discussion can influence the decision a great deal. Most of us think we control less than we do, and we influence less than we can. Could the opposite of that be true? It certainly is in this case.

I'd also like to tell you about what I observed about your behavior. First, you got emotional and said it couldn't be done. I think you are selling yourself short, because you have a good mind, and you can do a better job of bringing your expertise and charisma to the decision-making process. People will listen to you. I sense your resistance, and it frustrates me. You have great potential, and I'd like to see you grow.

I would also suggest you bring your expertise and some solid evidence to your conversations and build your case for the changes you want. Can I make a suggestion? (David waits for a nod.) In the future, don't discount the impact you can have on this team in a positive way. Are we in sync? (David waits for an acknowledgment.)

I'd like you to focus more on what brought us to our conclusion. Start asking yourself what behaviors you need to do more of, less of, what you would like to see start, and what needs to stop. And, ask the same of me.

A number of things are important to take away from this conversation. By changing how we think, process information, and our behavior, we can help human beings get out of negative patterns. Some of the categories important to think about include:

- Get out of the usual conversational dance.
- Create a *Safe Space* in which conversations end in productive outcomes.
- Don't make the conversation predictable.
- Use questions that can reframe the conversation when you sense they are not going in a productive direction.
- Use questions that can keep the conversation solution focused.
- Create a space for the person to respond in a different way and stop and think, not just react.

Very early in this book, we discussed Stephen Covey's concept of stimulus and response. Human beings learn to react quickly to certain types of stimuli. Fortunately, humans can also learn to react differently. You, as a leader, can allow individuals the space to think differently simply by changing what that stimulus is. By changing the modality of how you engage in conversations, outcomes can change for the better. In our example with David and Adam, the whole conversation changed by using *Innovative Questions*.

An Apology

There's another aspect of turning it around that we would like to discuss here. We previously spoke of the power of an apology in other situations. An apology can also go a long way to changing the outcome of a difficult situation.

In this case study, we talk about dealing with apologies from other individuals. Other individuals often use the apology as a catchphrase or cliché: Words without meaning. And, that can create a situation filled with anger. In these cases, we recommend drilling down into the cliché to find out what's actually going on.

Story: Being Late

One of Chris's clients, Greg, was very upset when he called Chris one day because a highly paid consultant was late to a meeting, and it was delaying the rest of his day. Greg wanted to take the consultant to task over what she had done. He knew, however, that a confrontation would set the wrong tone for the rest of the meeting, in addition to making everyone feel stressed and upset.

Chris had another idea. He said, "Greg, can I make a suggestion?" Greg replied, "Of course." Chris went on, "What do you think she is going to say when she comes in the door?" Greg replied, "I'm sorry I was late."

"You are probably right," said Chris, "Does that mean anything to you?" "No, she does this all the time," said Greg. "Right again. So why don't you try this, say, *'Apology Accepted.'* Then, when she says something like, "'It won't happen again,' you can say 'Thank you.'" Mission accomplished.

Sure enough, the consultant was late and apologized. Greg said, "Apology accepted," which caused the consultant to pause. It wasn't what she expected, and the outcome changed. She said it wouldn't happen again, and Greg said, "Thank you." Tipping point: Little things can make a big difference, and words have meanings.

David's team was so struck by this example that they tried it themselves. Once again, as we have been advocating throughout this book, a simple step had great impact.

The conversation was similar. It went like this:

Vendor: I'm sorry I didn't meet the deadline.

Manager: Apology accepted. Thank you.

Vendor: (Pauses) I'm truly sorry. I was getting ready to go on vacation for the first time in two years, and I just overcommitted. It will not happen again.

Manager: I understand, and I agree.

This conversation exhibits what we are repeatedly conveying — take an example *Innovative Question* and try it. That's what happened here. And it worked.

Conclusion

Remember; in the arsenal of changing the way people engage with you, it is not that difficult to try some new steps. It's simple and very powerful. All you have to do is remember and then, as the Nike commercial says, "Just do it!"

Innovative Questions, as we've shown in this chapter, do allow you to turn around the situation. You can change your interactions from negative to positive, and your outcomes can improve dramatically.

Things you can do....

Use one of the following IQs to change the tone of an angry situation:

- Whatever part I had in creating this, please accept my apology. It was not my intention. (Optionally add: I commit to do better with your help.)
- Going forward, what do you need more of? Less of? What do you need to start? What should stop?
- How can I help make this better?
- What were you hoping I could do for you?

Try to speak for two or three minutes, and then ask people to comment on what you just said.

At the end of each meeting, ask yourself if you tried one new *Innovative Question.*

Doing the Job

We hope that we have made a convincing argument for you to try *Innovative Questions*. Additionally, we hope that once you try *Innovative Questions*, you find them to be as effective as we, our clients, and our teams have found them. We firmly believe that once you have embraced *Innovative Questions*, you and your team will get better at getting to the best decisions possible. Remember, though, there are a number of things that need to be in place for *Innovative Questions* to work.

In the first appendix, we've established a job description for leaders that indicates the skills and abilities needed for *Innovative Questions* to work well and skills to avoid while practicing them.

Additionally, because change for the better is sustained only when it is practiced, we've included a sample daily sheet in Appendix B for helping you embrace *Innovative Questions* and incorporate them into your daily routine. You should fill out this daily sheet each day and see if you are progressing in using the strategies we have outlined in this book. We know this will be an effective reminder of what you need to do to improve your interactions with others.

We want to remind you of Cicero's definition of a statesman/leader versus a politician. The leader possesses the following four attributes:

1. A bedrock of principles
2. A strong moral compass
3. A clear vision for where they want to go
4. The ability to communicate that vision so people buy into it and will follow their lead.

Innovative Questions work only when you start with the bedrock of principles. They then allow you to create a *Safe Space,* where people buy into you as a leader, are safe to express themselves, and are willing to follow your lead.

Also remember that each of your team members is at different stages of *readiness* and *willingness* to do their work. Remember to assess your team members for *readiness* so that you use questions that support the ability, *readiness* and *willingness* of each of your team members.

We've created the following diagram to help you see a number of the *Innovative Questions* forces at work all at once:

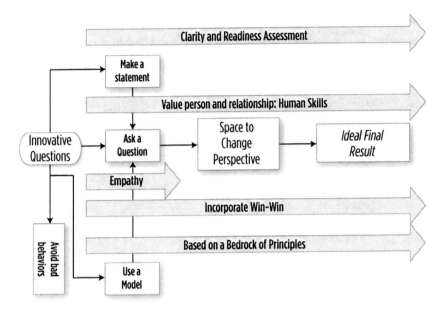

Figure 13.1

Innovative Questions start by working toward clarity on the outcome and targeting questions at the appropriate level of the individual with whom you're working. They require empathy, an understanding of human need, and a true desire to see everyone win with the outcome. Of course, all of this relies on the concepts that Cicero defined more than two thousand years ago: A bedrock of principles.

With these themes in place, *Innovative Questions* are very simple. Use a question, make a statement, or use one of the models we've defined to open a space for your conversational partners to make better decisions in reaching each *Ideal Final Result*. By using *Innovative Questions*, not only do you create a more positive perception of you, team members are more able and willing to implement a joint vision and do it happily. Finally, by asking questions that change the perception that others have of you, you will be more readily able to turn conflict into positive outcomes. We hope that you will start by taking the simple step of trying just one or two of the things you have learned from this book.

Job Description for the Leader

The most important single ingredient in the formula of success is knowing how to get along with people.

— THEODORE ROOSEVELT

This appendix provides a job description for the leader. According to Cicero, a leader is one who is capable of defining a vision and can motivate people to execute on that vision. In order for *Innovative Questions* to work, the following are necessary components.

Innate Abilities:
- A bedrock of principles.
- A strong moral compass.

Tasks and activities to accomplish:
- Support your team.
- Be there to help.
- Come from a place of integrity.

Requirements:
- Help and guide people to get what they need to be successful.

- Make sure that all process goals are met.
- Ensure that everyone gets an opportunity to express their goals and intents.
- Question team members' assumptions and beliefs.
- Determine what is right about an idea first.
- Find common ground.
- Make sure that improvements fit the needs of the individual and connect to their wider world.
- Hold people appropriately accountable.
- Know when it's important for you to win personally.

People need to see you as:
- On their side.
- Willing to ask questions and not tell them the answers.
- Willing to challenge thinking, including your own.
- Not willing to put others down.
- Willing to think through their and others' ideas.
- Acting as an ally to the team.
- Helping the team think things through.
- Helping the team get better.

Good skills to have:
- Help your team see the benefit of behaving nicely.
- Get along with others.
- Create synergy.
- Empathy: understand from their point of view.
- Pay undivided attention.
- Listen actively.
- Interpret others' intentions.
- Build on "becauses."
- Use "and."

Skills to avoid:

- Huge ego.
- Needing to win.
- Being overly competitive.
- Making excuses for poor behavior.
- Winning at all costs.
- Not letting others talk or express their points of view.
- Always having the last word.
- Using the words "but," "however," and "in spite of."

Sample Daily Sheet

In order to help you implement change, it's important to check in every day on the area on which you want to improve to make sure that you are staying on track. Chris uses this tool with every one of his clients.

It's pretty simple. Simply ask yourself one or more of the following questions each day, and put a check mark in the day of the week if you've executed on that item. If you don't like the tasks we've put down, pick your own. As long as you are working on it every day, you will get better.

Task	M	T	W	Th	F
Did I ask an *Innovative Question* today?					
Did I exhibit behavior with a strong moral compass based on a bedrock of principles today?					
Did I strive for clarity today?					
Did I assess *readiness* today?					
Did I look for a win-win solution today?					
Did I come across as trying to help today?					
Did I help create a Safe Space for others today?					
Did I seek to find common ground today?					
Did I work to achieve an *Ideal Final Result* today?					

Innovative Questions

Here is a list of *Innovative Questions* that you can use as you are working with others.

Category	Sub-category	Question / Statement
Question	AAR	1. What did you set out to do?
Question	AAR	2. What actually happened?
Question	AAR	3. How did it happen?
Question	AAR	4. If you could do it again, how would you do it differently?
Question	AAR	4. What insights do you have?
Question	AAR	5. What are you going to do moving forward?
Question	Asking opinions	How well do I do that?
Question	Asking permission	Can I be the devil's advocate for a moment?

Question	Asking permission	Can I give you a suggestion?
Question	Axiom	Are you pulling someone toward you or pushing them away?
Question	Axiom	How much time do we spend trying to get someone to do something that's important to you?
Question	Axiom	What's your premise?
Question	Behavioral rehearsal	How are you going to start this conversation?
Question	Change	Have you noticed a difference?
Question	Change	You know I've been trying to change and work on [blank]. Have you noticed a difference?
Question	Clarity	Are we agreed on the outcome?
Question	Clarity	Correct me if I am wrong, but are we not in agreement on this?
Question	Clarity	What could go wrong?
Question	Coaching	Are you committed to changing?
Question	Coaching	Are you willing to change?
Question	Coaching	How much time over the course of a month would you be willing to devote to getting better at this?
Question	Coaching	In order to make a change, you need courage, discipline to follow through, and humility. Do you think you have these?
Question	Coaching	This takes courage. Do you think you're up to this?

Question	Coaching	This takes determination. Do you think you're up to this?
Question	Coaching	What are the good questions you ask?
Question	Coaching	What's a skill you'd like to be more effective at and perceived to be more effective at?
Question	Coaching	Where do you want to be in 3 to 5 years?
Question	Coaching	You've got to convince me you want to fly.
Question	Common ground	What can we agree on with what we just discussed?
Question	Common ground	What do we both need for this to happen?
Question	Common ground	What part of what I just said do you agree with?
Question	Feelings	Have you observed the other people in the room?
Question	Feelings	When someone else says ABC, what if you asked this question instead of jumping down their throat?
Question	General	Are you open to thinking about it a different way?
Question	General	At what cost would you achieve this goal?
Question	General	Can I make a suggestion in getting this project done?
Question	General	Can we agree that we are truly going to collaborate and come up with the best possible decision?
Question	General	Can you commit to getting to me in the event that you are running into any issues?

Question	General	Do you need anything from me?
Question	General	Do you realize in the last 5 min. you said, "That's great, but" five times. Can I call you on it?
Question	General	Do you think you need to listen to them to understand what they can do for you, or do you just know that?
Question	General	Do you understand that if something is not going the way we discussed, you need to get to me right away?
Question	General	Have you thought about asking the question a different way?
Question	General	How are you connecting the dots?
Question	General	How confident are you that you will be able to complete this project on time?
Question	General	How confident are you, on a scale from 1 to 10, that you will get to me if there is a problem?
Question	General	How do you like to learn?
Question	General	How do you want to check in with me?
Question	General	How good do you want to be?
Question	General	How important is it for you to get better at this?
Question	General	How long are you going to allow for this to go on?
Question	General	How long has it been a problem?
Question	General	If anything could go wrong with this idea, what would it be?

Question	General	If I wasn't there, what would you do?
Question	General	If you could wave a magic wand and change whatever you could about the situation, what would you do?
Question	General	If you do this well, what's the upside for you?
Question	General	I'm sensing that you are reluctant to do this project? Is that an accurate statement?
Question	General	Is it negotiable?
Question	General	Is that statement relevant?
Question	General	Is this a crisis?
Question	General	Is this the most effective way to go about it?
Question	General	Is what I'm saying making sense?
Question	General	Just to make sure we are on the same page; Are you comfortable with coming to me after each task is completed?
Question	General	On a scale of 1 to 10, how confident are you that you are capable of completing this project?
Question	General	Questions? Thoughts?
Question	General	Six whys: Keep asking why until you get to the root cause.
Question	General	Something is on my mind. Can I share it with you?
Question	General	Statement: I'm not very good. Response: Can you get better?

Question	General	What are you doing about it? The situation?
Question	General	What are you going to do over the next [timeframe] to be ready at the right time?
Question	General	What could you have done to be helpful?
Question	General	What do you need to do to get to the end result you desire?
Question	General	What evidence do you have to support that?
Question	General	What evidence do you have to support what you're saying right now?
Question	General	What is your plan?
Question	General	What part of that statement I just made is true?
Question	General	What part of what I just said do you agree with?
Question	General	What problems is this creating?
Question	General	What type of support would you like to have from me to get this project done?
Question	General	What types of ideas do you have for getting this project done?
Question	General	What would it take to motivate you to do this?
Question	General	What do you see as the implications of this?
Question	General	What's the premise from which you are coming?
Question	General	What's worked in the past for you?

Question	General	When are you going to do this?
Question	General	Where is your time better spent?
Question	General	Will you do it again?
Question	General	Would I be correct in assuming that's a "No"?
Question	Ideal Final Result	How do we define success?
Question	Ideal Final Result	What are the consequences for failure and success?
Question	Ideal Final Result	What is the ideal final result?
Question	Ideal Final Result	What measurements will we use along the way?
Question	Ideal Final Result	What resources are there?
Question	Ideal Final Result	Who is accountable for what?
Question	Magic Wand	Magic Wand: What's one skill you would like to improve?
Question	Scale	On a scale of 1 to 10, how committed are you to changing?
Question	Scale	On a scale of 1 to 10, how likely do you believe you will be on time with this project?
Question	Scale	On a scale of 1 to 10, how reluctant are you to implement my suggestion?
Question	Top 25	Are you open to changing your mind?
Question	Top 25	Can you help me understand how that works?

Question	Top 25	Could the opposite of what you just said be true?
Question	Top 25	Do you think that you have the potential to address this?
Question	Top 25	Do you want a suggestion? OR Can I offer a suggestion?
Question	Top 25	Help me understand how this gets us to the best possible decision.
Question	Top 25	How confident are you that you will complete this project on time and on budget?
Question	Top 25	How important is this to you? On a scale of 1 to 10?
Question	Top 25	How much time have you spent thinking about this? OR How long have you been thinking about it?
Question	Top 25	How would you know if it's successful?
Question	Top 25	I agree with you on A, B, and C. On D, I see it differently. I don't see how D gets us from here to there. What am I missing?
Question	Top 25	I know you think this has not worked in the past, but if you could have a magic wand and make all of those problems disappear, how would you do this? OR ...but what if all of those political, budgetary, and other problems were erased? How would you make this happen?
Question	Top 25	If I gave you new information, would you change your mind? OR If I presented facts and information to the contrary, would you change your mind?
Question	Top 25	Is it possible that the opposite of what you're saying is true?

Question	Top 25	Is that accurate? OR Is that an accurate statement on my part?
Question	Top 25	It sounds like no matter what I say, your mind is made up. Is that accurate?
Question	Top 25	Let me ask you a question.
Question	Top 25	On a scale of 1 to 10...
Question	Top 25	What do you need from me?
Question	Top 25	What is the *ideal final result?*
Question	Top 25	What needs to start/stop in order to free you to make this happen?
Question	Top 25	What were you hoping I could do for you?
Question	Top 25	What would you like to see more of, less of? What would you like to see start, stop?
Question	Top 25	When you say [blank], what do you mean?
Question	Turning it around	Did what I said upset you?
Question	Turning it around	Get them to say "Yes." Ask them, "Can I offer a suggestion?"
Question	Turning it around	Give me an example of what you would like to see more of and less of. How do you think that would affect the outcome?
Question	Turning it around	I am getting the sense that your mind is made up and new information won't matter. Is that accurate?

Question	Turning it around	I can see that success on this issue is important to you. How can I help you achieve an outcome that would work for you?
Question	Turning it around	I don't want to fight you on this. What are you doing to improve?
Question	Turning it around	I get the sense that I'm upsetting you. Is that accurate?
Question	Turning it around	I get the sense that this doesn't interest you. Is that an accurate assessment?
Question	Turning it around	I see you as argumentative right now. Is that accurate?
Question	Turning it around	I'd like to get clearer on that. What's your intention?
Question	Turning it around	I'm getting the sense you like confrontation. Is that an accurate assessment?
Question	Turning it around	Let me ask you a question, right now. Are you angry?
Question	Turning it around	Let's say what I'm saying is true. Would you be willing to reconsider your point of view?
Question	Turning it around	Obviously, you're a big supporter of this cause. Give me a specific issue that you'd like to discuss. What about this specific item resonates with you?
Question	Turning it around	That's really interesting. Can I ask you a couple of questions? My understanding was something different.
Question	Turning it around	What do you think you should do to improve?
Question	Turning it around	What is your desired result? Please explain it to me.
Question	Turning it around	You seem to be uneasy about completing this project. Can you tell me if that's true?

Appendix C: Innovative Questions

Quotation	Spinoza	Judge a person by the questions they ask rather than their answers.
Statement	Axiom	Prefer common denominator to compromise.
Statement	Axiom	Acknowledge when someone's upset.
Statement	Axiom	Allow others to win as as often as you can.
Statement	Axiom	Always / never triggers an emotion to prove you wrong.
Statement	Axiom	Ask questions.
Statement	Axiom	Charm and a smile go a long way.
Statement	Axiom	Defer to someone else's point of view.
Statement	Axiom	Define success.
Statement	Axiom	Define the win-win.
Statement	Axiom	Don't make it more complex than it needs to be.
Statement	Axiom	Focus on interests, not just the issue.
Statement	Axiom	Forward looking, solution oriented
Statement	Axiom	I don't care, and I am not interested in the root cause.
Statement	Axiom	If I thought you meant to treat people with disrespect, I wouldn't work with you.
Statement	Axiom	If people think your mind is closed, they stop thinking.

Statement	Axiom	It takes one who is skilled at communication to change the course of a conversation.
Statement	Axiom	Listen for the words that lead to clarity.
Statement	Axiom	Listen to different points of view with an open mind.
Statement	Axiom	Look for common ground.
Statement	Axiom	Look for what you agree with.
Statement	Axiom	Look to defer to other people's points of view as often as you can.
Statement	Axiom	Make it safe to fail.
Statement	Axiom	Never say "role-play." People are averse to it.
Statement	Axiom	Prove the other person right.
Statement	Axiom	Reframe the situation.
Statement	Axiom	Seek first to understand.
Statement	Axiom	Tap into smart people's brains.
Statement	Axiom	Tell them a story about you.
Statement	Axiom	Words have meanings.
Statement	Axiom	You don't want to unnecessarily anger someone and push them away.
Statement	General	Convince me. I'm open.

Statement	General	Don't over-commit and under-deliver.
Statement	General	I don't see anywhere here where it says _____.
Statement	General	I want to reiterate that you will get to me if there is a problem.
Statement	General	If you are being bullied, say, "Let me finish."
Statement	General	I'm glad you stepped up.
Statement	General	I'm here to help you be more successful.
Statement	General	I'm just trying to get clear.
Statement	General	I'm not interested in getting into an essay.
Statement	General	Let me show you how I might do something like that.
Statement	General	Read this first one over, and tell me what you're willing to do.
Statement	General	That's a big word.
Statement	Ground rules	As the manager, from my perspective, your behavior was inappropriate.
Statement	Ground rules	If this behavior continues, you won't get my recommendation.
Statement	Ground rules	In all candor, here is what you need to develop.
Statement	Ground rules	Let me be clear: That behavior wasn't okay OR Here are my expectations.
Statement	Ground rules	Let me give you the reasons I think you should do this.

Statement	Ground rules	Next meeting: No talking.
Statement	Ground rules	On this team, these are the norms by which we operate. Would you like to discuss them? Is there anything you'd like to add to these?
Statement	Ground rules	These are some things you do well; here are some things to work on.
Statement	Ground rules	This behavior needs to stop.
Statement	Ground rules	This is nonnegotiable.
Statement	Ground rules	This is what I need.
Statement	Ground rules	This is what I would like you to do.
Statement	Learning moment	As you move through your career, you're going to encounter stuff like this.
Statement	Learning moment	Before we break, I want to revisit what just happened.
Statement	Learning moment	I also think that this will be a very important skill for you to have in your arsenal.
Statement	Learning moment	I expect you to be capable of thinking beyond that which you see as a roadblock.
Statement	Learning moment	I think you are selling yourself short, because you have a good mind, and you can do better.
Statement	Learning moment	I want to point out to you that you were able to resolve the issue by thinking differently.
Statement	Learning moment	I'd also like to tell you about what I observed about your behavior.
Statement	Learning moment	I'd like you to focus more on what brought us to our conclusion.

Statement	Learning moment	Start asking yourself what behaviors you need to do more of, less of, what you would like to see start, and what needs to stop.
Statement	Statements to avoid	Adding too much value.
Statement	Statements to avoid	Blaming others.
Statement	Statements to avoid	Don't say there's nothing to get upset about.
Statement	Statements to avoid	I'm confused.
Statement	Statements to avoid	It always does.
Statement	Statements to avoid	It never does.
Statement	Statements to avoid	Passing judgement.
Statement	Statements to avoid	Showing how smart you are.
Statement	Statements to avoid	There's nothing to get upset about.
Statement	Statements to avoid	Winning too much.
Statement	Top 25	I'm here to help.
Statement	Top 25	Let me be clear.
Statement	Turning around	The quality of your excuses is exquisite.
Statement	Turning it around	Humor me.

Statement	Turning it around	I am certain that you can prove yourself right.
Statement	Turning it around	I get the sense what I'm saying is not even registering with you. Is that accurate?
Statement	Turning it around	I get the sense you like to stick it to people often. Is that accurate?
Statement	Turning it around	I hear you telling me that you cannot do this. I'm certain that you can make that a self-fulfilling prophecy.
Statement	Turning it around	I would love for you to be right. Convince me.
Statement	Turning it around	I'm certain you can make that a self-fulfilling prophecy.
Statement	Turning it around	I'm getting the feeling that...
Statement	Turning it around	I'm just telling you how I interpret it.
Statement	Turning it around	I'm sitting here trying to think if I should rephrase the question so you'll answer it on my third attempt.
Statement	Turning it around	Let me tell you how you are coming across to me right now.
Statement	Turning it around	Let me tell you what I have to see to get you what you want.
Statement	Turning it around	Say more.
Statement	Turning it around	For someone with your self-esteem, I'm shocked at your reluctance to try this.
Statement	Turning it around	The arguments you are using are circular reasoning.

Statement	Turning it around	The way you express yourself inhibits other people from participating in the process. I'd like to ask you not to do that.
Statement	Turning it around	To me, everything boils down to performance.
Statement	Turning it around	We're not going to leave here until we have a satisfactory answer going forward.
Statement	Turning it around	Whatever part I had in creating this, please accept my apology. It was not my intention.
Statement	Turning it around	When you do this and challenge me, this is how it makes me feel.
Statement	Turning it around	You know that I'm working on this.
Statement	Turning it around	You're blowing smoke at me.
Statement	Turning it around	You've got to get over it.
Things to Do	Axiom	Add to others' ideas.
Things to Do	Axiom	Answers make an argument stronger or weaker.
Things to Do	Axiom	Are you pulling someone toward you or pushing them away?
Things to Do	Axiom	Ask an innocent/dumb question that makes someone think about what they just said.
Things to Do	Axiom	Ask, don't tell.
Things to Do	Axiom	Determine what is right about an idea first.
Things to Do	Axiom	Do not confuse knowledge with wisdom.

Things to Do	Axiom	Fundamental attribution error: We tend to blame our environment or other factors for our failures. For their failures, we tend to blame the person, their intelligence, or their character.
Things to Do	Axiom	Get clarity on the desired result.
Things to Do	Axiom	Give specific examples, not a laundry list. I have others — would you like more?
Things to Do	Axiom	Great storytellers tell stories that are relevant to the listener.
Things to Do	Axiom	It's all about action.
Things to Do	Axiom	Little things can make a difference.
Things to Do	Axiom	Start with what you agree with.
Things to Do	Axiom	Subscribe to a thoughtful publication that infuriates you.
Things to Do	Axiom	The most powerful way to influence is to ask questions and not telling.
Things to Do	Axiom	When behavior is inappropriate, you need to act.
Things to Do	Axiom	Words are important.

CPSIA information can be obtained
at www.ICGtesting.com
Printed in the USA
LVOW08s1158100517
533995LV00014B/606/P